A PORTRAIT OF THE
THEATRE

A PORTRAIT OF THE
THEATRE

BY FREDERIC OHRINGER

WITH INTRODUCTION BY
JOSEPH PAPP

© MERRITT PUBLISHING COMPANY LIMITED
TORONTO

(ISBN 0-517-53928-4)

ACKNOWLEDGMENTS

Joseph Papp   Edgar Cowan

Edwina von Gal
Sara Ohringer

George Adams,   Stephen Novick   Brian O'Neill
Paul Martino   Nancy Heller   John Springer

Sheldon Seidler   Helen Hans
Simon Dring   Jordan Bojilov

William Atkinson

William Hicks   Nuala FitzGerald
Michele Theriot   Stephen Morris   Timothy Chandler

Luke Wynne   Griffin Smith   Hector Ruiz

SAMUEL J. OHRINGER, my father

CONTENTS

INTRODUCTION

When I first met Fred Ohringer in June of 1973, he had just returned from Bangladesh, a second tour I learned, with a heavy portfolio of portrait photographs. A bearded young man in his late 20's, he was shy but intense, hesitant but persistent in his request for a showing at the Public Theatre.

He had covered the war in Bangladesh from its beginning. After it was over, he returned with a number of magazine assignments to photograph more of the same: human tragedies, the crippled and the dead.

I looked at his face. He was pale and nervous. His eyes were filled with the horrors he had seen through the distance of a viewfinder. The camera had always stood between him and his subject, and this fact bothered him. He felt a need to make amends for protecting himself from direct exposure to misery by means of a camera. His conscience laid bare by this realization, Ohringer had returned to Bangladesh, not as a photo-journalist but as a portrait photographer.

I asked him why. "By isolating the subject from his environment", he told me, "I would be forced to really look at the person I was photographing. The subject would no longer be an object. I had begun to see photo-journalism as an invasion of privacy, voyeurism of the worst kind, the exploitation of another's ill fortune. It was a dehumanizing experience."

Ohringer spoke rapidly, hesitating from time to time to find the proper word, as the photographs came out of his portfolio. In front of me, strewn on the floor, were some of the most stunning portraits I had ever seen. A handsome Bangladesh woman, majestic, strong and warm. Another, which hangs in my office, is of six men, beggarly in appearance but proud of their bearing. Their faces are generous and expressive.

When asked who these men are, I sometimes reply, "Our Board of Directors". The truth in this jest is that Ohringer had captured the distinction and stature beneath the external appearance. In over a hundred photographs, from the poorest man to the Prime Minister, I was impressed by Ohringer's ability to see beyond class barriers. He had sought and found the nobility in a people, dignified in their misery and determined to survive.

I found in Ohringer a mixture of artistic striving, social consciousness and the recognizable urge of those of us in this book who seek self-expression through a connection with others. Prior to our meeting, Ohringer had no interest in the theatre. I became his first major contact, and as a result, he was introduced to the people working at the New York Shakespeare Festival—the actors, authors, designers, and directors who have found a kind of home at the Public Theatre.

It is a theatre full of life and also marked by a strong concern for social issues. He very much related to that. The same impulses which bring people to the theatre as a profession, the need for intimacy and connection, were present in Ohringer. "Portrait photography", he told me, "is the most direct, the most connected photographic discipline—a liaison between the sitter and the photographer". He was seeking the straight-out relationship of portraiture, of talking specifically to one person. Ohringer needed to turn his lens away from scenes of death to portraits of the living.

On the day I arrived at Ohringer's to sit for my portrait, I entered through a black door (which I remember as being red) and climbed to the top of the stairs. The studio setting is totally unlike a theatrical situation, somewhat like a hospital. You're there to have your head x-rayed. Although the photographer is in charge, he assumes the role of serving his subject. He appears to be at your command, and he is humble and gentle.

There is a certain nervousness about being photographed which anyone would have, and Ohringer exploits that. He acts as a comforting force, the doctor in the hospital. You're nervous to know what the result of these x-rays is going to be, an x-ray which will expose something on the inside, not revealed on the outside. A mechanical procedure is taking place.

But even while the photographer is making adjustments, he is bobbing his head in and out from behind the camera and carrying on a conversation. You need to be spoken to, to have a hand extended which you can reach out and touch. And this makes you feel somewhat secure. Although the circumstance is nerve-wracking, the photographer is not a threat. He is a calming influence on the front line.

As I look at the portraits in this book, I am not particularly struck by the fact that they are all people of the theatre, many of them performers. When you put an actor in front of a camera for a publicity photograph, he will respond as a character in the play and with an awareness, because he constantly functions that way, of people watching him. In most of these photos, it's as though the subject is alone, left to his own devices, and someone came along and put a frame around his or her face. Ohringer captures a moment when their defences are down, and they're not trying to impress anyone. He reveals a side of these people that is not ordinarily shown to the outside. It's the side of you that you have by yourself.

To have the subject relate to him in this way, Ohringer disengages the clutch and photographs in neutral. On the part of many of the people in this book, there's a consciousness of that. They know that's happening and give themselves to the situation. There's no defense against it, because there they are, doing nothing—just sitting.

What's extraordinary is the way Ohringer is able to be with these people without their being concerned or intimidated by his presence. He exists, simply, as a factor of the situation. This establishes a connection which makes the person quite natural. Not natural as I know most of these people, when they are involved in the day to day life of the working process, but natural in the sense of not being viewed by anybody, just as you never think of the way you look when you're alone or occupied with something.

Viewing this collection of photographs, I am reminded of Henry Luce, publisher of TIME and LIFE, who used to insist that all pictures be shot head-on, so people would see the eyes. You have that here. Most of the subjects are looking straight at you. But these are not candids. There is a formality in portraiture, a stylistic factor which freezes an attitude rather than seeing it in motion. Portrait photography reveals an aspect of the character which epitomizes the way the photographer sees his subject. It's like saying give me one word for this person, and that's the shot you take. It's very hard to sum someone up in a single word. What Ohringer chooses for his point of focus—whether photographing people in the theatre or people in Bangladesh—is his perception of the strongest aspect in the character of his subject.

Theatre is thought of as essentially artificial, as a reproduction of life situations. And what strikes me in these photos is that people in the theatre are no different from any one else. Many people in the theatre are quite ordinary. They lead simple lives, sometimes much simpler than those who come to watch them perform. But the general public wants the illusion of the movie star. They want to see the actor as he was in the movies. There's nothing illusionary about these photographs. They're forthright, open and demonstrate the dignity and strength of their subject.

Before there were cameras, the only people who could afford to have their portraits painted were the very wealthy. Portraiture. There's class in portraiture. Here we have a portrait gallery of people in the theatre (often considered the world's second oldest profession) dignified by Ohringer's ability to crystallize each person's strong points, the best in his or her character.

The mere assemblage of many of the outstanding people in the American theatre makes this a book about the theatre. But it's also, and to my way of thinking, more importantly, a book about people. Ohringer makes no distinction between people in the theatre and people out of the theatre. People in Bangladesh. People in New York. His approach is the same. He looks for their strength, not their weakness, not their everyday attitude, but the moment when, alone, they reveal the heart inside.

Joe Papp

JOSEPH PAPP

A PORTRAIT OF THE
THEATRE

I can only tell you that I have enjoyed life, largely, I think, because writing and directing has always seemed like play to me.

I love the stage and I feel homesick when I am away from it for too long. If I do my work well, some truth that the playwright wishes to express, be it large or small, is transmitted through me to the hearts and minds of the audiences and sometimes changes are made there. This is enormously exciting... It means that art is politics, that our art is revolutionary, and because theatre is in the avant garde, that we effect cultural change. I am a catalyst.

RICHARD RODGERS, 1979

The only difference between doing
"I Remember Mama" (1979) and the first "Garrick Gaieties" (1925)
is 54 years.

HUME CRONYN, JESSICA TANDY, 1978

Why do I act? I'm not sure I do. I've always thought of myself
as a performer. An entertainer.

MARYBETH HURT, 1979

Dancing is very hard and its rewards are very strange—very
personal. But work has been very loyal to me, so I'm willingly
very loyal to work.

JULIE HARRIS, 1974

EDWIN SHERIN, 1979

The rigors of the theatre give me the means to define who I am and the victories have always been sweet. But it is a war; a war between what is and what's dreamed of. Directing, more or less, permits a choice of one's comrades-in-arms.

I have to respect anybody who can write a good play, and the
contemporary playwright I admire the most is Lanford Wilson.
The person I would most like to write a play for is Luchiano Pavarotti.

I am fond of all characters in all of my plays, and my only
favorite is George Topax in *The Revenge Of The Space Pandas*.

JEROME ROBBINS, 1978

For the past twelve years I have concentrated on choreographing ballets. During this period people have constantly asked me when I was going to work in the theatre again. I always find this very curious because there, I feel, is where I have been working.

TAMMY GRIMES, 1979

Re: My Daughter, Amanda Plummer—
Durango Mexico—5:30 am Breakfast
—Filming *Cattle Annie and Little Britches*
She eats hard scrambled eggs—
2 pieces of buttered toast-tea-orange juice
Radiant-alive-eyes clear-face still soft from slumber—
no signs of tired
Beautiful; she talks in fast rhythms—
Now she goes—I kiss her good-bye
her hair an angry black cloud
framing her fierce strong features
her silhouette caught
shimmering in the Durango sun
She turns and waves to me at the door
She is going to work—
She belongs to the world
and things will never be quite the same
She is an actress...
I can't think of a more fulfilling life
than the one she has chosen for herself
...but I am prejudiced—

MICHAEL MORIARTY, 1976

38

BARRY BOSTWICK, 1976

The hardest thing to learn about show business is patience
. . . the second hardest is a good hobby.

JOHN SPRINGER, 1979

I faced up to the fact that I'd never be an actor. Producer?
Tried and failed. Writer... Oh, occasionally. But where could I
fit in the world I love most... the world of theatre and films...
And even perhaps make a contribution? That's how
theatre/film publicity-P.R. came into my life. How wonderful
when your love becomes your life.

How do I feel about the theatre? I'll tell you: if this picture looks envious, it's because I've just seen Sweeney Todd.

MAUREEN STAPLETON, 1979

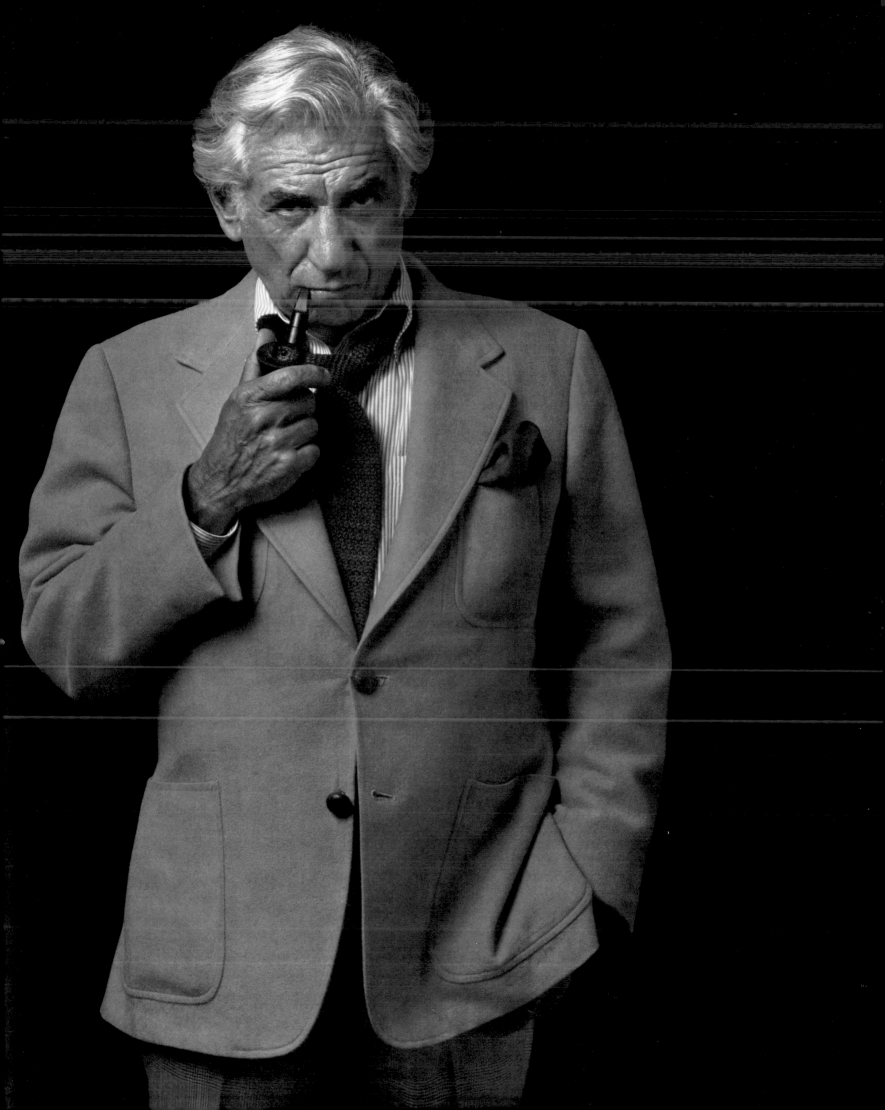

The critic is a link between the artist and the audience. The artist is a synthesist. He takes his view of life, his own experience and his own genetic makeup and from all this, creates a work of art. The critic is an analyst. He looks at the work of art from the viewpoint of his own persona. Like Hamlet's crab he goes backwards. He uses his own life experience and being to provide an insightful view of what the artist created. The artist comments on life through art. The critic comments on art through life. His commentary should be informed with knowledge and experience. The critic is a symbiotic parasite on the underbelly of art. Not totally essential —but hopefully helpful.

I wanted to be a theatre critic since the age of 14. It was my destiny. I have no creative or interpretative abilities. I am not a frustrated playwright, actor, choreographer, director or dancer. I am simply a totally fulfilled critic. To paraphrase Anatole France, I have the privilege of recounting the adventures of my soul in a parade of masterpieces. But why paraphrase, or even translate Anatole France. *Le bon critique est celui qui raconte les aventures de son ame au milieu des chefs d'oeuvre.* That is my aspiration—and, for that matter my job.

I am often asked what is my favorite play and I never have one. What is your favorite flower? Your favorite girl's name? Even your favorite girl? No, these do not exist. They are whims and fancies... eddies of memory in a sea of time.

But what was your most memorable performance? It is curious that as you get older you remember the past with a frightening, almost an accusing clarity. So many performances ... with actors and actresses, to say nothing of singers and dancers, tugging petulantly at the cloak of memory. But, one performance? Well, it was really two.

Laurence Olivier in 1945 in a double bill as Mr. Puff in Sheridan's *The Critic.* And as Oedipus in Sophocles' *Oedipus Rex.* I saw the program, at London's New Theatre with the Old Vic Company, some six seven or eight times. At the time, oddly enough, I never realized how great Olivier was. He was an actor I always resisted. He seemed too technical. His Richard III, his button moulder in *Peer Gynt* (and Richardson was the peerless Peer), all his acting seemed at that moment of delivery, too delivered, too contrived. Yet looking back on Olivier's performances, and, yes, particularly, in this bizarre and besotted double-bill, they remain etched by acid in my memory.

As Puff, it was perhaps the way he floated his hand, a needless gesticulation of wind and fancy, and, of course, as Oedipus it was that cry of pain from a wound self-inflicted and atavistic, a savage man desperately screaming his blind way into a realization of meaningless reality. Yes – it was Olivier.

It is easy to put down the facts of one's activity in the theatre, but it is difficult to describe one's feeling, which involves more than what one has actually achieved. I entered the theatre out of no search for ego gratification or hope for personal achievement. The theatre has always functioned as the mirror of civilization. My work was directed not towards achievement, flattering as that may be, but from the very beginning, involved working with others to stimulate them towards a realization of what the theatre could represent and a recognition of the responsibility that they owed to their talent. I had not always anticipated the level to which they would rise. I have been both surprised and gratified by their subsequent success, though I have been upset by some of the failures which were not always due to the lack of talent. Talent may be a natural attribute but it cannot fully assert itself without being nurtured, stimulated, trained and given the opportunity to function. The search for talent has been the most satisfying part of my activity and will remain so. But I must admit to a degree of personal satisfaction at being able to illustrate and make use of my teaching in my recent jump from teacher to performer. This was unexpected but not difficult and has given me a measure of ego gratification.

Acting, which has always held the mirror up to nature, has been essentially the same throughout the ages. Attitudes towards acting, and styles of acting may change, but the process of acting brings one closest to man and human understanding.

ALFRED de LIAGRE, JR., 1979

The first fifty years are probably the hardest
but I still find the theatre the most fascinating, excruciating,
unpredictable adventure in the world.

MADELINE KAHN, 1978

JACK GILFORD, 1979

JOEL GREY, 1978

To be asked to direct the dazzling talents of Miss Minelli and then to have the unexpected joy of appearing opposite her on stage made for just about the most exciting time in my career.

ANITA GILLETTE, 1978

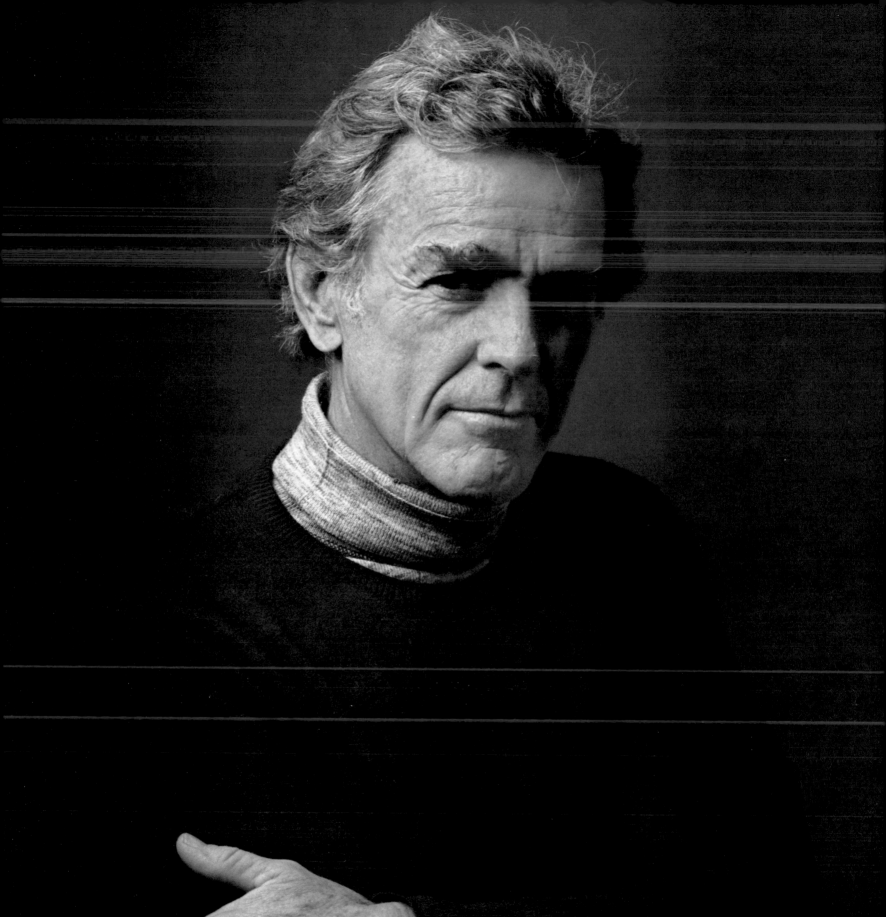

Q. Do you want to move your audience?
A. Yes. From one place to another.

SWOOZIE KURTZ, 1979

The Acting Company... to create a strong American theatre.

Anybody can tell you what a costume designer does in the theatre. Almost anybody, that is, except producers and their "angels". When examining the sometimes enormous budgetary demands of a Broadway play or musical, the eyes of the producer and his backers dilate and tear when they come upon the costume costs. The question that follows is one that I have actually heard so often that I am no longer amused at its naivete, "Good heavens! Why so much money for clothes?" From that moment on the designer will spend the better part of her working days on the phone trying to explain basic economics. It is during these times that a degree in cost accounting seems more useful than any design talent. Even after the enormity of the task is made clear to them, and the costumes are finally designed, constructed and on the stage, the wardrobe is still singled out as the root of all evil. The following are comments heard during the try-out period of a musical deeply in trouble: "The show would be so much better if her dress was blue, her shoes beige and, please, no hat."; "And you know this dance number would bring the house down if the dresses were just a little shorter."; "Oh darling, remind me to bring my sweater from home—it would make this actor look much more comfortable."; "Don't you think we can shop for some of these things tomorrow." (The show was, mind you, a 1905 period piece.) Why, one asks, does one continue in a business pervaded by such juvenile idiocy? Once in a while, there comes along an assignment that makes it all worth while. The beauty of a "Great Gatsby", the excitement of a "Chorus Line", the joy of "Annie" and the fulfillment of a "Ballroom" fill one with a sense of enormous accomplishment and pride. More than that, there are those rare, exceptional people who give joy to the work and to life; that extraordinary man, Joe Papp, to whom I literally owe my career; the collaborative genius of Michael Bennett, whose taste and talent can fill the working day with pleasure; Bernie Gersten, whose love and support are unending. Then in my own special world, the costume shop, the artistry of Milo Morrow and Ray Diffen; the exquisite talent and infinite patience of Barbara Matera and her staff; the exacting eyes of Woody Shelp; and the knowledge and loyalty of Donna Tomas. I have worked with the best, and that includes my agent-friend, Ed Bondi. As for future plans, Joe Papp promised me a rose garden.

Suffice it to say I love what I do. I've been lucky in being able to do it a lot lately and in response to your question re: theatre vs. film; no – it's not likely I'll neglect one for the love of the other—they have such different personalities.

Succinctly put, light is my life. Light shows me all the things about life and, in short, how could one live and/or experience life without light. If this sounds convoluted, I suppose that is how we think about light as related to life.

Now you ask me about working with Michael Bennett. I could, and maybe will, write a book on this some day. Meanwhile, may I just say that Michael understands to the maximum what light can do to help him say what he is trying to say... whether it is verbally or musically... and we do seem to be on the same wavelength.

As to my favorite show, or what show I would like to have worked on, my favorite show is any Michael Bennett show, and if there is a Michael Bennett show that I have not worked on then that is the show I would like to have done. We have a love for the theatre, and for each other, that seems to be able to be transmitted by light.

MICHAEL BENNETT, 1975

Love Life,
Live.

LIV ULLMANN, 1974

Acting is knowing how to suggest a character, and at the same time,
finding it all in your own heart.

I really have nothing to say about acting, theatre, and life.
Whenever I say something about them I feel I'm limiting them
to something. At their greatest, acting, theatre, and life emerge
from nothing. And, of course, that's something.

VINCENT SARDI, 1975

The theatre and the people involved in it
have been home and family to the Sardis.
That is why I, in turn,
try to make Sardi's a club and home
for theatre people.

73

JOHN CULLUM, 1978

GWEN VERDON, 1979
This looks the way I feel.
I wish everybody would accept me this way
instead of always expecting,
—*Broadway's Darling.*

DAVID RABE, 1974

ARVIN BROWN, 1978

I love the theatre because it's a contact sport: Actor to Actor,
Actor to Audience, and best of all Audience to Actor.
What other medium in our passive society asks you to
reach out at least part-way for your entertainment? The Actor
may not come to you unless he knows you want him;
the relationship is short, intense, and if you're both lucky,
might reveal just a corner of the human soul.

One of the questions most frequently asked of me is: do I ever get blocks? I have had enough blocks to fill in from 23rd Street to 89th Street. My blocks usually come about mid-way through the first act of a play. It's about this point that I begin to get nervous and ask myself, "Is this good enough to go on with, to spend another three or four months writing and another six months in re-writing, casting, rehearsing and going through the agonies of a production?" Usually at that point I will put the work aside and let it sit for six weeks or six months... (even for six years but it has to be on a very low flame) and then go on to some other project. Then I will take it out and read it again. Sometimes I will be delighted and surprised at what I read and want to get at it again immediately. *Barefoot In The Park* and *The Sunshine Boys* sat in that drawer for over a year, rapping on the wood and squealing in a tiny voice to be let out. *God's Favorite* was in there for three years. I have one now called, *Brighton Beach Memoirs*, that has come out and gone back in for over four years now. And some just sit in that manuscript *Graveyard* forever. I have the beginnings of well over twenty to thirty new plays that will age and mummify like King Tut, but alas, will never have his world wide audience.

The plays that wrote "straight through" were *California Suite, Chapter Two, The Odd Couple* and *The Gingerbread Lady*. (For the last one, I rented a tiny room in the Plaza Hotel because I was stuck on the third act, and didn't come out for a week. The room service equalled my eventual royalties.)

The longest writing time was for my first play, *Come Blow Your Horn.* It took three years and twenty complete revisions from page one on. What's this? I just opened my drawer and found something I started two years ago. Hmm, this looks interesting. Excuse me, I have to get back to work...

In the U.S.A., ca. 1979, *A Portrait Of The Theatre* would be of a theatre divided by classes—of a useless Broadway theatre, corporate fat and idea lean—an "Off Broadway Theatre", foundation fat and fascinating as anything really boring—and a theatre that yet will come, whose barest outline causes excitement. A revolutionary theatre, an anti-imperialist theatre, a people's theatre, which will rise again, but this time stay and chronicle the end of one social system and the struggle, rise and life of a more advanced social system.

I would have liked my music to be discussed
during the tennis games between Gershwin and Schonberg.

I love being in the theatre because it makes me happy.

I hate looking at photos of myself
—they rob me of the illusion that I'm a new
up and coming person in show business.

WOODIE KING, JR., 1978

I love the theatre! It is a part of my life. I don't think I could live
without it. The black theatre comes out of my blackness and
my knowledge of black people's hopes, fears, and desires. It is
an American experience in a beautiful and artistic form.

When not directing I can be found at Yankee Stadium during baseball season and at Madison Square Gardens during the winter. There I see the best theatre in the world. No sport *escapes my interest.*

GORDON DAVIDSON, 1979

The theatre—the work of theatre artists—dramatic literature—represents for me a primary way in which we know who and what and why we are. It gives visual and aural meaning to ideas and emotions and behaviour.

I have devoted my life to the making of theatre which demands as much of its audience as it does from its artists. I have searched in my work to define and re-define in contemporary terms how a sense of community can be established in the theatre. I know that what happens on stage must be a truer reflection of what is happening in life and that the audience sitting in the theatre be a truer representation of our vast and non-homogeneous society—that the mixture of age, race, sex, language and economic disparities all contribute vitality and energy to be shared by all.

My life's work in art and my life's work in the world is not work based on hits, box office or even awards—but rather on respect for the truth and for the imperfections which make us unique in time and at the same moment part of a great continuum.

JASON ROBARDS, 1974

LYNN REDGRAVE, 1974

True, I've worked on Broadway, for Papp, and downtown at my own "off-off" Ontological-Hysteric. Obviously I was doing work closest to me at my own theatre, where I can take all the time I need for preparation and deny myself nothing that I think is aesthetically necessary. Then, as you move upwards, more and more compromises have to be made, for economic reasons (in my experiences) only. That is to say—the set for *3-Penny* had to be cut in half from our original designs. On the other hand, Joe Papp had faith in what we were doing and allowed previews and rehearsals to continue long after the announced opening date—the same with Stuart Ostrow and Lynn Austin—which is simply to say I've been lucky in having strong-willed producers of taste and determination. The truth of the matter is I find little difference, no matter where I work. People care, people try to do their best, there are *always* horrendous problems because making art (if it's any good) always involves having something be "bad" before it gets "good". You simply have to be prepared for that, and not lose heart.

It remains true, however, that my work at Ontological-Hysteric Theatre can (largely because of economic considerations) be much more complex and intricate than work uptown. And of course—much more intellectual and idiosyncratic—which is my reason for being an artist. So to answer question *#2*—Ontological-Hysteric work *should* be seen on Broadway—because it's the *best* work of an artist (me) who's had, I guess, some success uptown with—let's face it—work that is not really his *very* best, most significant work. Should be seen—but *could* be seen? Well, obviously, the situation on Broadway is such that not much of interest can be done there these days.

Your last question, other directors whose work I admire. From the past—Joan Littlewood and Judith Malina were the two directors (in the far back days when I used to see lots of theatre) who's work always interested and stimulated me. Then—that elusive American genius Jack Smith who I think is the source of most of what's interesting in avant-garde theatre today, and finally the opulent work (though I think a bit misguidedly over-chic) of the French director Patrice Chereau.

An actor (offstage or screen) tends to be like anyone else: a private person without a public personality. To be photographed while acting is part of his professional life; to be photographed while sitting on a stool in someone's studio is puzzling, confusing, bewildering.

What to do? Invent a character, become for the moment someone who is an aspect, a facet of yourself like a chip of mirror on one of those reflecting glass spheres that, spinning over a ballroom, cast countless beams of light and create about them a spurious sense of gaiety. Thus an actor about to be "immortalized" on film must convincingly smile, frown, look pensive or lighthearted and so on. In short he is still acting, and since it is a performance frozen in its particular mood (there is no second act, no subsequent scene, no follow up dialogue) it is, until the shutter clicks, perpetuation of that instant which the photographer (director) and the subject (actor) have agreed is appropriate. It is a technique which all public figures sooner or later must master. All the worlds' a stage, etc....

SANTO LOQUASTO, 1978

There is a recollected moment of contact between the
stage and the audience which, however rare, is what you try to
capture for yourself as well as for the public—perhaps more
for yourself.

ROBERT PATRICK, 1979

Joe Cino's Caffe Cino was the first place in world history
where plays were presented without regard for economic,
box-office, critical, academic, esthetic, religious, military, politi-
cal, literary, legal, or social standards, that is, as works of art, an
idea that has spread everywhere and will be the artistic and
philosophical capital of theatre for centuries to come.

CLEAVON LITTLE, 1974

...The theatre is my native habitat
and the company of players affords me endless delights...

ZOE CALDWELL, 1974

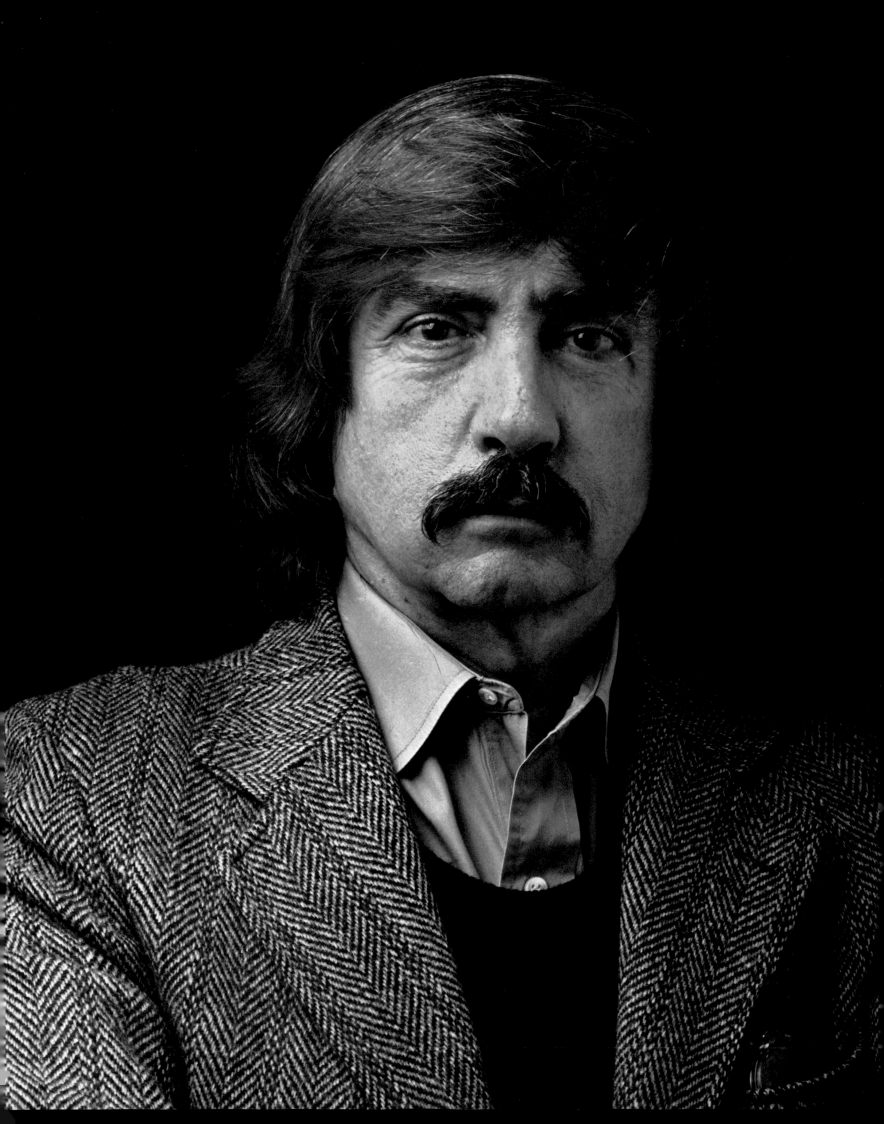

EDWARD ALBEE, 1979

No posed photograph is an objective record of its subject; it probably is of its taker, though.

The professional photographer imposes his subjective view on the emanations and disguises of his subject, and emerges with a mutually agreeable artifice.

Since—as some societies have it—we lose a part of our soul to each photograph, it is as well that art intercedes in this portioning.

I think the reason that people who are photographed frequently are so particular about the result is that they realize they have come to resemble their photographs, unlike the uncelebrated whose photographs, happily, still bear some resemblance to how they actually look.

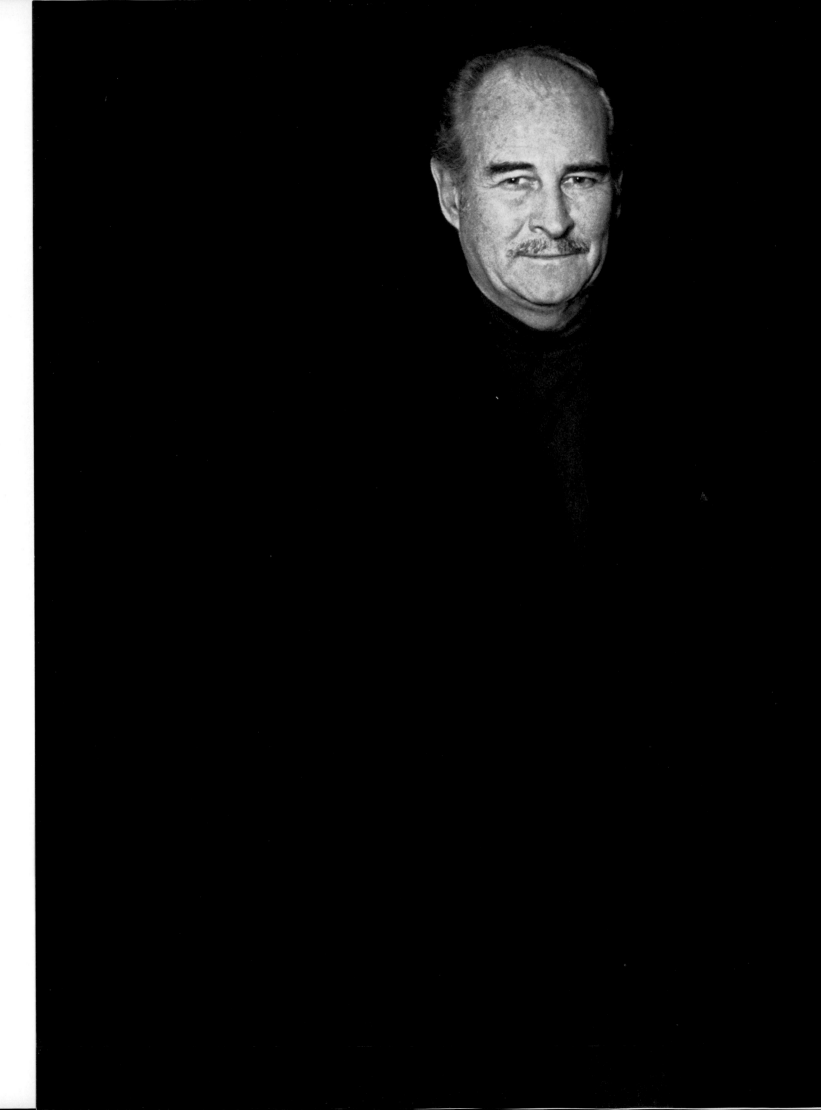

JOHN LITHGOW, 1979

I am just one man doing the best he can. I never thought of what it takes to make a great play. You have to love to write. You must not make yourself do it. I only worry about what I will write today. I'll be dictating on my deathbed.

The constant need to take yourself to the center of all pain, joy and despair, the looking into and experiencing emotion, raw, the public bleeding, exposing your secrets unashamedly, is both the curse and blessing of the actor-artist. It forces you to deal every day with insanity, tamper with your own psyche and enter into a world beyond your control. For this commitment society should be grateful. A true and visionary actor can expose the best and the worst of us, and if we are able to accept his perception we can make the next step toward enlightenment.

THOMAS BABE, 1976

What I want to happen on the stage
are the coincidences of reality gathered together
in a highly unlikely but satisfying shape.

LAWRENCE KORNFELD, 1979

REVEREND AL CARMINES, 1979

In musical theatre we sing about the pain in our life.
And in the singing is life.

ROBERT BRUSTEIN, 1974

JOSEPH CHAIKIN, 1979

Questions of character: whom do you see when you look at me? Whom do you think I see when I look at you? Who or what is it that you think cannot be seen by anyone? Is it still you? What bits of information would be used to publicly describe you? Does each piece of information have a value attached to it? What amount of memory, would you say, determines how you will continue? Would you say that there are parts of yourself which have not lived yet? What would bring forth the life of those parts?

HAROLD CLURMAN, 1974

I have been involved in the theatre for fifty-five years as actor, stage manager, playreader, producer, director, critic, teacher, lecturer, author and despite all trials and tribulations, inevitable in all worthy enterprises, I must confess that I enjoyed every minute of those years at work.

HENRY FONDA, 1978

When I was an unaware kid fresh out of college, I was pushed
into a community stage play. The pusher was a family friend
named Doe Brando (who later had a son named Marlon). I
consider it to be the most important "push" of my life. As a
shy, self-conscious young man, I learned I could hide behind
the mask of a character I would play. I still do that and I'm
happier and more secure in public as Tom Joad or Mr. Roberts
or Clarence Darrow or Justice Dan Snow than I ever could be
as just Henry Fonda.

ANGELA LANSBURY, 1979

Regarding the audience—what was once considered carriage trade has now broadened its base and engages the attention of every ethnic group. Attendance is up. So are prices. Curiously, this current great influx of theatre — going (which ignores the center city blight) is largely attributable to television. Using the medium for advertising, the theatre has attracted a television audience and playing to this audience has lowered our standards.

Regarding the critics—the standard of theatrical criticism has also lowered over the years and the public perceives this. Consequently, the influence of reviewers has diminished. Since we have fewer outlets, we have fewer writers, and very few of those can be taken seriously. Some reviewers simply use the legitimate theatre as platforms for self-aggrandizement, and this I deplore.

Regarding the producers—to be a producer requires taste, organizational ability, money or access to it, and a fair amount of luck. Very few contemporary producers possess all those ingredients. There are several producers whose major concern is quality, who realize that "if it isn't on the page, it isn't on the stage." A theatrical producer has an advantage over a television or film producer in that he really is the final arbiter of the taste and quality of what he produces. We are fortunate to function in an area of the arts where, when a producer is convinced that his show isn't good enough for Broadway, he can close it in Boston. The veteran producer understands that you are going to strike out some of the time and when that happens you must wait for your next turn at bat.

HOROVITZ: Why I write plays.
Growing up Jewish in Wakefield, Massachusetts, seemed to provide the necessary childhood problems to support the impulse too skitted to the edge of matters, and to write.

At age seven, I wrote a sketch about an overzealous dentist extracting my chiclet, which was cheered and praised by my peers.

At age thirteen, I completed a novel, called *Steinberg, Sex And The Saint,* which I mailed off to New York, to a major publisher. The manuscript was rejected, but praised for its ''wonderful childlike quality.'' Having suffered such indignity of rejection and of critical slur, I returned to the drama and completed, at age seventeen, my first full play, entitled, not surprisingly, *The Comeback.* This play was immediately produced in Boston in University Productions that starred a young actor who bore a remarkable resemblance to the author, but whose name was Jefferson Parrish, in January; Arthur Phillips, in March; and in retirement, by May. Once again, peers praised and cheered.

Since age seventeen, (I am, at this writing, age forty), I have written an embarrassing number of plays. I don't know how many, precisely. It is certain, however, that I have written one play too many. The question is: which one?

PETER EVANS, 1978

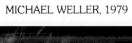

MICHAEL WELLER, 1979

IRENE WORTH, 1977

ROBIN WAGNER, 1978

BARNARD HUGHES, 1979

I've been an actor all my life, and I feel privileged to be one. I think acting is an important, contributing, exciting way to spend your life. The trick is to make your life and your career come out even.

ESTELLE PARSONS, 1978

Your portrait, unlike any other of me, is truly my actress self— waiting, undefined, unkempt, uncertain, restless, resonating, with a need to be taken over by the figment of a playwright's imagination. I don't know this self I see in your portrait. I have only felt its existence inside me. It is usually not seen in this waiting state . . . my acting instrument.

Each of us is hoping the other is about to have an idea.

The theatre in 1979 is an integrated world that has achieved
current popularity through friendly inter-relationships between
all of its components—Broadway, regional, experimental and
university. It is moving into the next decade as a publicly
accepted force in the world of culture, economic stimulation
and urban improvement.

TONY WALTON, 1979

Each production requires its own special visual alphabet. It would be wonderful to be able to forget almost all previous design experience in approaching each new project and try for a fresh response.

ROBERT LEWIS, 1978

One of my favorite quotes on acting is called "Demands of the Actor in Ancient India": "Freshness, beauty, a pleasant broad face, red lips, beautiful teeth, a neck round as a bracelet, beautifully formed hands, graceful build, powerful hips, charm, grace, dignity, nobility, pride, not to speak of the quality of talent".

ELLIS RABB, 1979

ELI WALLACH, ANNE JACKSON, 1978

A statement which relates to feelings about acting, theatre, or
life in general sends the head spinning. If one were to put it
succinctly it would come out like this: acting in theatre is our
life.

I'm grateful to the theatre for allowing me to put new expression into music and I am very moved by the spirits and imaginations of the actors and musicians who are working with me to break down boring old traditions and to build a new musical theatre.

TOM ALDREDGE, 1979

Since there was nothing in my early background
to point to a career in theatre,
I'm constantly waiting for *them* to discover
that it's all been a hoax...

An appointment in time with the senses.

SYLVIA SIDNEY, 1977

I was a teenage girl in films and theatre...And now I'm a
character actress. It's the world's roughest gamble where
you're unemployed 50% of your life. I can't get sentimental
about the theatre...But the years have gone by and I'm still a
part of it.

SAM WATERSTON, 1975

ROBERT PRESTON, 1978

I was born and had ten years of real life and, at that early age,
knew it could be better. From that day to this, it has been. I'll
live other people's real lives and hide my own.

MORTON GOTTLIEB, 1979

If mankind is the first order of life to reflect upon itself,
the theatre is its reflector.

BIOGRAPHIES

GEORGE ABBOTT
Producer, Director, Author
Born: June 25, 1887; Forestville, New York

Producer/Author/Director: *Lily Turner*, 1932; *Heat Lightning* (Co-Author, Co-Producer), 1933; *Sweet River*, 1936; *Boys From Syracuse*, 1938; *Beat The Band* (Co-Author), 1942; *A Tree Grows In Brooklyn* (Co-Author), 1951.

Author/Director: *Four Walls* (Co-Author), 1927; *Three Men On A Horse* (Co-Author), 1935; *Where's Charley*, 1948; *The Pajama Game* (Co-Author, Co-Director), 1954; *Damn Yankees* (Co-Author), 1955; *New Girl In Town*, 1957; *Fiorello* (Co-Author), 1959; *Tenderloin* (Co-Author), 1960; *Flora The Red Menace* (Co-Author), 1965; *Anya* (Co-Author), 1965; *Music Is*, 1976.

Producer/Director: *The Drums Begin*, 1933; *John Brown*, 1933; *Kill That Storey* (Co-Producer), 1934; *Boy Meets Girl*, 1935; *Brother Rat*, 1936; *Room Service*, 1937; *Angle Island*, 1937; *Brown Sugar*, 1937; *All That Glitters*, 1938; *Pal Joey*, 1940; *Kiss And Tell*, 1943; *Get Away Old Man*, 1943; *Snafu*, 1943; *It Takes Two* (Co-Producer), 1947; *Barefoot Boy With Cheek*, 1947; *Look Ma, I'm Dancin'*, 1948; *Mrs. Gibbon's Boys*, 1949; *In Any Language* (Co-Producer), 1952.

Director: *On The Town*, 1944; *Billion Dollar Baby*, 1945; *High Button Shoes*, 1947; *Call Me Madam*, 1950; *Wonderful Town*, 1953; *Once Upon A Mattress*, 1959; *Take Her, She's Mine*, 1961; *A Funny Thing Happened On The Way To The Forum*, 1962; *Never Too Late*, 1962; *How Now, Dow Jones*, 1967; *The Education Of H*Y*M*A*N*K*A*P*L*A*N*, 1968; *Three Men On A Horse* (revival), 1969; *Pajama Game* (revival), 1969; *Life With Father* (revival), 1974; *Winning Isn't Everything*, 1978.

Also: directed over ten films including *All Quiet On The Western Front*, *Pajama Game* and *Damn Yankees*.

Awards: Pulitzer Prize — *Fiorello*; Tony Awards — *Fiorello* (director), *A Funny Thing Happened On The Way To The Forum* (director); NY Drama Critics Awards — *Fiorello*, *Wonderful Town*; Donaldson Awards (director) — *Billion Dollar Baby*, *High Button Shoes*, *Wonderful Town*, *Pajama Game*.

EDWARD ALBEE, *Playwright*
Born: March 12, 1928; Washington, D.C.

One Act Plays: *The Zoo Story*, 1959 (Schiller Theatre, Berlin), (Provincetown Playhouse; Arts Theatre, London, 1960); *The Death Of Bessie Smith*, 1960 (Schlosspark Theatre, Berlin), (York Playhouse, 1961); *The Sandbox*, 1960 (Jazz Gallery); *Fam and Yam*, 1960 (White Barn, Westport); *The American Dream*, 1961 (York Playhouse).

Broadway: *Who's Afraid Of Virginia Woolf?*, 1962, 1976 (London, 1964); *The Ballard Of The Sad Cafe* (adaptation), 1964; *Tiny Alice*, 1964; *Malcolm* (adaptation), 1966; *A Delicate Balance*, 1966; *Everthing In The Garden* (adaptation), 1967; *Box/Quotations From Chairman Mao Tse-Tung*, 1968; *All Over*, 1971; *Seascape* (also director), 1975.

Also: Founder, with Richard Barr and Clinton Wilder, of Playwrights Unit and producer (also with Barr and Wilder) of numerous productions at the Cherry Lane Theatre.

Awards: Vernon Rice and Obie Award — *Zoo Story*; Tony Award, NY Drama Critics Award, Outer Circle Critics Award — *Who's Afraid Of Virginia Woolf?*; Pulitzer Prizes — *A Delicate Balance*, *Seascape*; Margo Jones Award (with Barr and Wilder); elected to the National Institute of Arts and Letters.

THEONI V. ALDREDGE,
Costume Designer
Born: Salonika, Greece

Theatre Companies: For the New York Shakespeare Festival since 1960 over thirty Free Shakespeare plays in Central Park and Mobile Theatre productions; over twenty-five plays at the Public Theatre; Lincoln Center costume designs include *Boom Boom Room*, 1973; *The Au Pair Man*, 1974; *Dance Of Death*, 1974; *The Trelawny Of The Wells*, 1975; *Mrs. Warren's Profession*, 1976; *Threepenny Opera*, 1976; Festival Broadway productions of *Two Gentlemen of Verona*, 1971; *Sticks and Bones*, 1971; *Much Ado About Nothing*, 1972; *That Championship Season*, 1973; *A Chorus Line*, 1975.

Broadway: Over 100 productions including *I Can Get It For You Wholesale*, 1962; *Who's Afraid Of Virginia Woolf?*, 1962; *Strange Interlude*, 1962; *Any Wednesday*, 1964; *Anyone Can Whistle*, 1964; *Luv*, 1964; *Skyscraper*, 1965; *Cactus Flower*, 1965; *A Delicate Balance*, 1966; *You Know I Can't Hear You When The Water's Running*, 1967; *Illya, Darling*, 1967; *Little Murders*, 1967; *Hair*, 1967; *I Never Sang For My Father*, 1967; *Billy*, 1969; *The Sign In Sidney Brustein's Window*, 1972;

Find Your Way Home, 1974; *In Praise Of Love,* 1974; *Eccentricities Of A Nightingale,* 1976; *The Belle Of Amherst,* 1977; *Annie,* 1977; *Ballroom,* 1978; *I Remember Mama,* 1979.

Also: several films including *The Great Gatsby, Harry And Walter Go To New York, Network.*

Awards: Tony Award —*Annie;* Drama Desk Awards *Peer Gynt, Two Gentlemen of Verona, Much Ado About Nothing;* Maharam Awards — *Peer Gynt, Much Ado About Nothing;* Academy (Oscar) Award — *The Great Gatsby.*

TOM ALDREDGE, *Actor*
Born: February 28, 1928; Dayton, Ohio
Broadway: *The Nervous Set,* 1959; *Between Two Thieves,* 1960; *UTBU,* 1966; *Slapstick Tragedy,* 1966; *Everything In The Garden,* 1967; *Indians,* 1969; *The Engagement Baby,* 1970; *How The Other Half Loves,* 1971; *Rex,* 1976; *Vieux Carre,* 1977.
Off-Broadway: *Electra,* 1958; *The Butter And Egg Man,* 1966.
Theatre Companies: Goodman Memorial Theatre — *Hamlet,* 1950. New York Shakespeare Festival — *Henry V,* 1960; *Love's Labour's Lost,* 1965; *Troilus And Cressida,* 1965; *Measure For Measure,* 1966; *Richard III,* 1966; *Ergo,* 1968; *Romeo And Juliet,* 1968; *Twelfth Night,* 1969; *Cymbeline,* 1971; *Sticks And Bones,* 1971 (also Broadway, 1972); *Hamlet,* 1972; *The Orphan,* 1973; *King Lear,* 1973; *The Leaf People,* 1975. American Shakespeare Festival Theatre — *A Midsummer Night's Dream, Antigone, The Merchant Of Venice* and *Macbeth,* 1967. LaMama, ETC—*Stock Up On Pepper 'Cause Turkey's Going To War,* 1967; *Circle In The Square* — *The Iceman Cometh,* 1973; *Where's Charley,* 1974. Phoenix Theatre — *Canadian Gothic/American Modern,* 1976. Hudson Guild—*On Golden Pond,* 1978 (also Broadway), 1979.
Also: *The Boys In The Band* (London), 1969; directed *The Happiness Cage* (New York Shakespeare Festival), 1970.

JANE ALEXANDER, *Actor*
Born: October 28, 1939;
       Boston, Massachusetts
Theatre Companies: Charles Playhouse — *The Madwoman Of Chaillot,* 1965; Arena Stage — resident member, 1966-68 and guest

artist, 1970-71; over twenty-five productions including *The Crucible, The Three Sisters, Sergeant Musgrave's Dance, The Great White Hope* (also Broadway), *Mother Courage.* American Shakespeare Theatre — *Mourning Becomes Electra,* 1971; *The Merry Wives Of Windsor,* 1971; *Major Barbara,* 1972.
Broadway: *6 Rms Riv Vu,* 1972; *Find Your Way Home,* 1974; *First Monday In October,* 1978.
Also: appeared in the film of *The Great White Hope;* television appearances include *Eleanor And Franklin.*
Awards: Tony Award — *The Great White Hope.*

MAUREEN ANDERMAN, *Actor*
Born: October 26, 1946; Detroit, Michigan
Theatre Companies: American Shakespeare Festival — 1970, 1971 seasons. Arena Stage — 1971-72 season. Goodman Theatre — *A Doll's House,* 1973-74. Meadowbrook Theatre — *As You Like It,* 1974. Guthrie Theatre — 1974-75 season. New York Shakespeare Festival — *Hamlet,* 1975. Hartford Stage Company — *Listening, A History Of The American Film* (also Broadway, 1978), 1976-77. San Diego Shakespeare Festival — 1977. Phoenix Theatre — *The Elusive Angel,* 1978.
Broadway: *An Evening With Richard Nixon And...,* 1972; *The Last Of Mrs. Lincoln,* 1972; *Seascape,* 1965; *Who's Afraid Of Virginia Woolf?,* 1976.
Also: *Moonchildren* (Off-Broadway), 1972.

BORIS ARONSON, *Set and Costume Designer*
Born: October 15, 1900; Kiev, Russia
Broadway: Sets and Costumes — various productions including *The Merchant Of Yonkers,* 1938; *Mlle. Colombe,* 1954; *The Master Builder,* 1955; *Bus Stop,* 1955; *A View From The Bridge* and *A Memory Of Two Mondays,* 1955; *The Diary Of Anne Frank,* 1955; *The Price,* 1968. Sets — over sixty productions including *Walk A Little Faster,* 1932; *Three Men On A Horse,* 1935; *Awake And Sing,* 1935; *The Body Beautiful,* 1935; *Paradise Lost,* 1935; *R.U.R.,* 1943; *South Pacific,* 1943; *Sadie Thompson,* 1944; *Detective Story,* 1949; *Season In The Sun,* 1950; *The Country Girl,* 1950; *The Rose Tattoo,* 1951; *I Am A Camera,* 1951; *I've Got Sixpence,* 1952; *The Crucible,* 1953; *A Hole In The*

Head, 1957; *Orpheus Descending*, 1957; *A Loss Of Roses*, 1959; *A Gift Of Time*, 1962; *Fiddler On The Roof*, 1964; *Cabaret*, 1966; *Zorba*, 1968; *Company*, 1970; *Follies*, 1971; *The Creation Of The World And Other Business*, 1972; *The Great God Brown*, 1973; *A Little Night Music*, 1973; *Dreyfuss In Rehearsal*, 1974; *Pacific Overtures*, 1976.

Also: designs for the Yiddish Theatre, 1924-30; Radio City Music Hall stage productions, 1935; designs for Ballet Theatre, Ballet Russe de Monte Carlo, New York City Ballet and the Eliot Feld Ballet; Coriolanus Shakespeare Memorial Theatre, England), 1959; *Incident At Vichy* (ANTA, Washington Sq.), 1964; *Morning Becomes Electra* (Metropolitan Opera House), 1967.

Published Works; Marc Chagall, Modern Graphic Art.

Awards: Tony Awards — *The Rose Tattoo, The Country Girl, Season In The Sun, Cabaret, Zorba, Company, Follies, Pacific Overtures;* Maharam Award — *Cabaret;* American Theatre Wing Award — stage design, 1950-51.

ELIZABETH ASHLEY, *Actor*
Born: August 30, 1939; Ocala, Florida

Broadway: *The Highest Tree*, 1959; *Take Her She's Mine*, 1961; *Barefoot In The Park*, 1963; *Ring Round The Bathtub*, 1972; *Cat On A Hot Tin Roof*, 1974; *The Skin Of Our Teeth*, 1975; *Legend*, 1976; *Caesar And Cleopatra*, 1977.

Also: *The Crucible* (Off-Broadway), 1959; *The Enchanted* (Kennedy Center), 1973; American Shakespeare Theatre, member 1974 season; *Carnival Dreams* (New Dramatists), 1978; films include *The Carpetbaggers, The Ship Of Fools, Rancho Deluxe, 92 In The Shade;* numerous televison appearances.

Awards: Tony Award — *Take Her She's Mine.*

TONY AZITO, *Actor*
Born: July 18, 1948; New York, New York

Theatre Companies: *Red, White And Black* (Player's Theatre), 1971; *Player's Project* (Repertory Theatre Of Lincoln Center), 1972; *Secrets Of The Citizens Correction Committee* (Theatre At St. Clement's), 1973; *Threepenny Opera* (New York Shakespeare Festival), 1976 (Lincoln Center) and 1977 (Delacorte Theatre); *Happy End* (Chelsea Theatre Centre, also Broadway), 1977.

THOMAS BABE, *Playwright*
Born: March 31, 1941; Buffalo, New York

Theatre Companies: New York Shakespeare Festival — *Kid Champion*, 1975; *Rebel Women*, 1976; *Fathers And Sons*, 1978; *Taken In Marriage*, 1979. Manhattan Theatre Club — *Billy Irish* (co-production with the NY Shakespeare Festival), 1977.

Also: wrote *Great Solo Town* and directed *Two Small Bodies* (Playwrights Horizon), 1977.

IMAMU AMIRI BARAKA, *Playwright*
Born: (LeRoi Jones) October 7, 1934; Newark, New Jersey

Plays: *A Good Girl Is Hard To Find* (Montclair, NJ), 1958; *Dante* (1961) also titled *The Eighth Ditch* (New Bowery Theatre), 1964; *Dutchman* (Playwrights Unit, also Off-Broadway), 1964; *The Baptism* (Writer's Stage), 1964; *The Slave and The Toilet* (Off-Broadway), 1964; *J-E-L-L-O* (Black Arts Repertory Theatre School), 1965; *Experimental Death Unit 1* (Off-Broadway), 1965; *Black Mass* (Newark, NJ), 1966; *Arm Yourself And Harm Yourself* (Newark), 1967; *Slaveship* (Newark, 1967 and Chelsea Theatre Center, 1969); *Mad Heart* (San Francisco), 1967; *Home On The Range* (Newark and New York City), 1968; *Great Goodness Of Life* (A Coon Show) (Off-Broadway), 1969; *Junkies Are Full Of (SHHH...)* and *Bloodrites* (Newark), 1970; *A Recent Killing* (New Federal Theatre), 1973; *Sidney Poet Heroical* (New Federal Theatre; also director), 1975.

Published Works: plays (in addition to some of the above) include *Police, The Death Of Malcolm X, BA-RA-KA; The System Of Dante's Hell* (novel); *Tales* (short stories); published volumes of poetry include *Preface To A Twenty Volume Suicide, The Dead Lecturer, Black Art, Black Magic, It's Nationtime, Spirit Reach.*

Also: Founder — American Theatre For Poets, Black Arts Repertory Theatre School, Spirit House (Newark); wrote the screenplay of *Dutchman.*

Awards: Obie Award — *Dutchman;* member of Black Academy Of Arts And Letters.

CLIVE BARNES, *Critic*
Born: May 13, 1927; London, England

Dance And Dancers: Assistant Editor, 1950-53; Associate Editor, 1961-65; New

York Editor, 1965. **London Daily Express:** music, drama, dance and film reviewer, 1956-65; **The Spectator:** Dance Critic, 1959-65; **New York Times:** Dance Critic, 1965-67; Drama and Dance Critic, 1967-77; **New York Post:** Dance and Drama Critic since 1977.
Author: *Ballet In Britain Since The War,* 1953; *Fred Ashton And His Ballet,* 1961; *Ballet Here And Now* (Co-Author), 1961; *Dance Scene, USA.*

MICHAEL BENNETT,
Director/Choreographer
Born: April 8, 1943; Buffalo, New York

Choreographer: *A Joyful Noise,* 1966; *Henry, Sweet Henry,* 1967; *Promises, Promises,* 1968; *Coco,* 1969; *Company,* 1970.
Director/Choreographer: *Follies* (co-director), 1972; *Seesaw* (co-choreographer, also author), 1974; *A Chorus Line* (co-choreographer, also conceived), 1975; *Ballroom* (co-choreographer, also producer), 1978.
Director: *Twigs,* 1973; *God's Favorite,* 1974.
Also: appeared as a dancer in *West Side Story* (National Tour), 1959 and on Broadway in *Subways Are For Sleeping,* 1961; *Here's Love,* 1963; *Bajour,* 1964. Choreographed the film *What's So Bad About Feeling Good.*
Awards: Tony Awards — *Follies* (co-director, choreographer), *Seesaw* (choreography), *A Chorus Line* (director, co-choreographer); *Ballroom* (co-choreographer); New York Drama Critics Award —*A Chorus Line.*

LEONARD BERNSTEIN, *Composer*
Born: August 25, 1918; Lawrence, Massachusetts

Broadway: *On The Town,* 1944; *Peter Pan,* 1950; *Wonderful Town,* 1953; *The Lark* (incidental music), 1955; *Candide,* 1956; *The First Born,* 1956; *West Side Story,* 1957; *1600 Pennsylvania Avenue,* 1976.
Also: Musical Conductor, New York Philharmonic — 1958-1969, named Laureate Conductor in 1969; conducted major orchestras in the United States and Europe; conducted at the Metropolitan Opera House and La Scala; Young People's Concerts and Leonard Berstein and the New York Philharmonic for televison; composer of various published works.
Author: *The Joy Of Music, Leonard Bernstein And The Young People's Concert, The Infinite Variety Of Music.*

Awards: Tony NY Drama Critics and Donaldson Awards —*Wonderful Town;* ANTA Citation; Emmy Awards for musical contribution to televison; Music Critics Award — *Jeremiah Symphony;* Alice M. Ditman Award, Albert Einstein Commemorative Award; Page One Award; American Symphony Orchestra Award; Christopher Award, Secondary Education Award —*The Joy Of Music.*

KERMIT BLOOMGARDEN, *Producer*
Born: Dec. 15, 1904; Brroklyn, New York
(Died: September 30, 1976)

Broadway: numerous productions including *Deep Are The Roots,* 1945; *Another Part Of The Forest,* 1946; *Command Decision,* 1947; *Death Of A Salesman,* 1949; *The Autumn Garden,* 1951; *The Crucible,* 1953; *Wedding Breakfast,* 1954; *A View From The Bridge,* 1955; *The Diary Of Anne Frank,* 1955; *The Lark,* 1955; *Most Happy Fella,* 1956; *Look Homeward Angle,* 1957; *The Music Man,* 1957; *The Gang's All Here,* 1959; *The Fighting Cock,* 1959; *Toys In The Attic,* 1960; *The Wall,* 1960; *The Gay Life,* 1961; *My Mother, My Father And Me,* 1963; *Anyone Can Whistle,* 1964; *The Playroom,* 1965; *Illya, Darling,* 1967; *Equus,* 1974; *Poor Murderer,* 1976.
Off-Broadway: *The Hot L Baltimore,* 1973; *Ionescapade,* 1974; *The Sea Horse,* 1974.
Awards: Tony Awards — *Death Of A Salesman, The Crucible, The Diary Of Anne Frank, Music Man, Equus;* New York Drama Critics Awards —*Death Of A Salesman, The Diary Of Anne Frank, Most Happy Fella, Look Homeward Angel, Music Man, Toys In The Attic;* Pulitzer Prizes — *Death Of A Salesman, The Diary Of Anne Frank, Look Homeward Angel;* Obie Award —*The Hot L Baltimore.*

BARRY BOSTWICK, *Actor*
Born: February 24, 1945; San Mateo, Calif.

Broadway: *Soon,* 1971; *Grease,* 1973; *The Robber Bridegroom,* 1976.
Theatre Companies: APA-Phoenix — *War And Peace,* 1967; *Pantagleize,* 1967; *The Misanthrope,* 1968; *Cock-A-Doddle-Dandy,* 1969; *Hamlet,* 1969. La Mama, ETC — *House Of Leather,* 1970; *Colette,* 1970. Chelsea Theatre Center — *The Screens,* 1971. Phoenix Theatre — *They Knew What They Wanted,* 1976.
Also: *Salvation* (Off-Broadway), 1969; films include *The Rocky Horror Show* and *Movie, Movie.*

Awards; Tony Award — *The Robber Bride-groom.*

LEE BREUER *Director*
Born: February 6, 1937; Los Angeles, Calif.

Mabou Mines: Founding Member, 1970; author/director *The Red Horse Animation* (premiere at the Guggernhein Museum), 1970; *The Saint And The Football Player,* in collaboration with Jack Thibeau, and *The B. Beaver Animation* (premiere at the NY Loeb Student Center), 1973; *The Shaggy Dog Animation* (New York Shakespeare Festival), 1978; *A Prelude To Death In Venice* (New York Shakespeare Festival), 1979; director *Come And Go* (premiere at the Brooklyn Bridge Festival), 1971; *Come And Go* (revised) and *Play* (premiere at LaMama, ETC), 1971; *The Lost Ones,* 1975, *Cascando,* 1976; collaborations include *Music For Voices* with Philip Glass, *Arc Welding Piece* with Jene Highstein, *Send/Receive/Send* with Keith Sonnier.
Also: directed at San Francisco Actors Workshop, 1963-65; studied with the Berliner Ensemble and Polish Laboratory Theatre; directed *Mother Courage* and *Play* in Paris and *The Messingkauf Dialogues* (Edinburgh Festival, 1968); advisor to American Indian Theatre Ensemble and Havajoland Outdoor Theatre.
Awards: Obie Award — Special Citation to Mabou Mines, 1975, *Shaggy Dog Animation* (also Soho Arts Award).

ARVIN BROWN, *Director*
Born: May 24, 1940; Los Angeles, California

Theatre Companies: Long Wharf Theatre — Artistic Director since 1967; directed over thirty productions including the American premieres of *A Whistle In The Dark,* 1968; (also Off-Broadway, 1969); *Country People,* 1970; *Yegar Bulichov,* 1970; *The Contractor,* 1971; *Solitaire/Double Solitaire* (world premiere, also Broadway), 1971; *The Changing Room* (also Broadway), 1972; *The Widowing Of Mrs. Holroyd,* 1973; *Forget-Me-Not Lane* (also at Mark Taper Forum), 1973; *Artichoke* (world premiere), 1975; also directed *The National Health* and *Ah Wilderness!* (also at Circle In The Square), 1974.
Also: *The Indian Wants The Bronx* (London premiere), 1967; (Broadway), 1970; *Long Day's Journey Into Night* (Off-Broadway), 1971; *St. Joan* (Ahmanson Theatre, LA), 1974; directed the film, *Cold Sweat* and

Forget-Me-Not Lane and *The Widowing Of Mrs. Holroyd* for television.
Awards: Vernon Rice Award — *Long Day's Journey Into Night.*

ROBERT BRUSTEIN, *Actor/Director/Critic*
Born: April 21, 1927; Brooklyn, New York

Theatre Companies: Yale Repertory Theatre — Founder, Artistic Director, 1966-79; supervised over sixty productions; appeared in *The Rivals, Watergate Classics, The Possessed, Troilus And Cressida, Ivanov;* directed *The Revenger's Tragedy, Macbeth, The Big House, Don Juan Or The Enemy Of God, The Wild Duck.* Harvard Loeb Drama Center — appointed Director, 1979.
Actor: over seventy roles in summer/winter stock and appearances in various television dramatic programs, 1950-57.
Critic: The New Republic (Drama Critic/Editor) 1957-67; New York Review Of Books (Cultural Critic), 1964-65.
Also: author of *Theatre Of Revolt, Seasons Of Discontent, The Third Theatre;* Dean of the Yale School Of Drama, 1966-79.
Awards: George Jean Nathan Award for Dramatic Criticism, 1962; George Polk Award for Criticism, 1965.

YUL BRYNNER, *Actor*
Born: June 15, 1915; Sakhalin, Japan

Broadway: *Lute Song,* 1946; *The King And I,* 1951; *Home Sweet Homer,* 1976; *The King And I,* 1977.
Also: *Twelfth Night* (The Little Theatre), 1941; *The Tidings Brought To Mary* (Barbizon Plaza Theatre), 1942; films include *The Ten Commandments, The King And I, Brothers Karamazov, The Sound And The Fury, Once More With Feeling, The Magnificent Seven, Taras Bulba, Invitation To A Gunfighter, Madwoman Of Chaillot.*

ZOE CALDWELL, *Actor*
Born: September 14, 1933;
      Hawthorn, Australia

Theatre Companies: Various roles with Union Theatre Repertory Company (Melbourne), 1953, 1962; Elizabethan Theatre Trust (Sydney), 1954, 1962; Royal Shakespeare Company, 1958, 1959; Royal Court Theatre, 1960, 1961; Stratford (Ontario) Shakespeare Festival, 1961, 1967; Manitoba Theatre Company, 1961, 1964; Guthrie

Theatre, 1963, 1965; Goodman Memorial Theatre (in *The Madwoman Of Chaillot*), 1964; Shaw Festival (Ontario), 1966; La Mama (in *Colette*), 1970; New York Shakespeare Festival at Lincoln Center (in *Dance Of Death*), 1974; Kennedy Center and Brooklyn Academy Of Music (in *Long Day's Journey Into Night*), 1975-76.

Broadway: *The Devils,* 1965; *Slapstick Tragedy* (Gnadiges Fraulein), 1966; *The Prime Of Miss Jean Brodie,* 1968; *The Creation Of The World And Other Business,* 1971.

Also: appeared on television in *The Apple Cart, Macbeth* and *Tragedy* and *The Prime Of Miss Jean Brodie;* Drama Desk Award — *Colette.*

LEN CARIOU, *Actor/Director*
Born: September 30, 1939; Winnipeg, Canada

Theatre Companies: Manitoba Theatre Center — various productions since 1961 including *Mr. Roberts, As You Like It, The Shoemaker's Holiday, The Skin Of Our Teeth, Mother Courage, The Taming Of The Shrew, Who's Afraid Of Virginia Woolf?, The Hostage, Andorra, The Tempest, The Threepenny Opera;* appointed Artistic Director, 1975. Stratford (Ontario) Shakespeare Festival — various productions 1961-65 including *The Tempest, Macbeth, Cyrano de Bergerac, The Taming Of The Shrew, Troilus And Cressida, The Comedy Of Errors, Timon Of Athens, Richard III, Le Bourgeois Gentilhomme, The Country Wife.* Guthrie Theatre — *The Skin Of Our Teeth,* 1966; *S.S. Glencairn,* 1966; *As You Like It,* 1966; *The Shoemaker's Holiday,* 1967; *The House Of Atreus* (also Broadway), 1967; *The Visit,* 1967; *Twelfth Night,* 1967; *The Diary Of A Scoundrel,* 1971; *Oedipus The King,* 1972; *King Lear,* 1974; named Associate Artistic Director, 1972. Goodman Theatre — *Othello,* 1968. American Shakespeare Festival — *Much Ado About Nothing, Henry V* (also Broadway) and *The Three Sisters,* 1969.

Broadway: *Applause,* 1970; *Night Watch,* 1972; *A Little Night Music,* 1973; *Sweeny Todd,* 1979.

Director: *Of Mice And Men,* 1972, and *The Crucible,* 1974 (Guthrie Theatre); *The Petrified Forest* (Off-Broadway), 1974; *Don't Call Back* (Broadway), 1975.

Awards: Tony Award — *Sweeny Todd.*

AL CARMINES, *Composer/Author/Lyricist/Actor*
Born: July 25, 1936; Hampton, Virginia

Judson Poet's Theatre: Director and Minister (of Judson Memorial Church) since 1961; composed music for *Vaudeville Skit,* 1962; *The Wax Engine,* 1963; *What Happened,* 1963; *An Old Tune,* 1963; *Home Movies* (also Off-Broadway), 1964; *Patter For A Soft Shoe Dance,* 1964; *Sing Ho For A Bear,* 1964; *Promenade,* 1965 (also Off-Broadway, 1969); *San Francisco's Burning,* 1967; *Song Of Songs,* 1967; *Gorilla Queen* (Co-Composer; also Off-Broadway), 1967; *Successful Life Of 3,* 1967; *Celebrations,* 1967; *In Circles (also Off-Broadway),* 1967; *Untitled Play,* 1967; *The Sayings Of Mao Tse-tung,* 1968; *The Line Of Least Existence,* 1968; *Peace,* 1968 (also Off-Broadway, 1969); *The Poor Little Match Girl,* 1968; *The Urban Crisis* (also author), 1969; *Christmas Rappings* (also director), 1969; *About Time* (also co-author), 1970; *The Playful Tyrant* (also author), 1970; *The Journey Of Snow White,* 1971; *Wanted* (also co-lyricist), 1971; *Joan* (also author, lyricist, director), 1971 (also Off-Broadway, 1972); *A Look At The Fifties,* 1972; *The Life Of A Man* (also author, lyricist, director), 1972; *The Making Of America,* 1972; *The Faggot* (also lyricist, director; also Off-Broadway), 1973; *Religion* (also author, director), 1973; *The Future* (also author, lyricist), 1974; *Listen To Me,* 1974; *Sacred And Profane Love* (also author, director), 1975; *Why I Love New York* (also author, lyricist), 1975.

Also: composer, author, lyricist of *The Duel* (Brooklyn Academy Of Music), 1974; appeared in *What Happened,* 1963; *Home Movies,* 1964; *In Circles,* 1967; *The Sayings of Mao Tse-tung,* 1968; *The Making Of America,* 1972; *Religion,* 1973.

Awards: Obie Awards — *What Happened, Home Movies, In Circles,* Special Obie to Judson Memorial Church, Special Obie for Sustained Achievement. Vernon Rice Award — *In Circles.* Drama Desk Award — *Peace, The Faggot.*

JOHN CAZALE *Actor*
Born: August 12, 1935; Boston, Mass.
(died; March 12, 1978)

Theatre Companies: Long Wharf Theatre — 1969-70, 1970-71, 1971-72 seasons. New York Shakespeare Festival — *The Resistable Rise Of Arturo Ui,* 1974; *The Local Stigmatic,*

1976; *Measure For Measure*, 1976. New Dramatists — The Wakefield Plays, 1976.
Off-Broadway: *The Indian Wants The Bronx*, 1968; Line, 1971.
Also: films include *The Godfather, Dog Day Afternoon, The Deer Hunter*.

JOSEPH CHAIKIN, *Actor/Director*
Born: Sept. 16, 1935; Brooklyn, New York
Theatre Companies: Living Theatre — member 1959-63 and appeared in *Tonight We Improvise*, 1959; *The Connection*, 1961; *Many Lovers*, 1961; *Man Is Man*, 1962. Open Theatre — founder and member 1963-73, appeared in *Endgame*, 1970 and directed *Terminal*, 1970; *The Serpent: A Ceremony*, 1970; *The Mutation Show*, 1972; *Nightwalk*, 1973; *Electra*, 1974. *Manhattan Theatre Club* — directed *The Seagull*, 1975. Mark Taper Forum — directed *Electra*, 1975-76 season. Theatre of Latin America — directed *Chile, Chile*, 1975. Shaliko Company— appeared in *Woyzeck*, 1976. New York Shakespeare Festival — directed *The Dybbuk*, 1978.
Off-Broadway: appeared in *The New Tenant* and *Victims of Duty*, 1964; *Sing To Me Thru Open Windows*, 1965; *The Exception And The Rule*, 1965; *Captain Fantastic Meets The Ectomorph*, 1966; directed interview part of *America Hurrah!*, 1966.
Author: *The Presence Of The Actor*
Awards: Obie Awards — Lifetime Achievement Award, *The Connection* (acting), *Man Is Man* (acting), *The Serpent* (to Open Theatre), *The Mutation Show* (best theatre piece); Vernon Rice and Drama Desk Awards — *The Mutation Show.*

GOWER CHAMPION, *Director/Choreographer*
Born: Geneva, Illinois; June 22, 1921
Broadway: Director/Choreographer — *Lend An Ear*, 1948; *Bye Bye Birdie*, 1960; *Carnival*, 1961; *Hello, Dolly*, 1964 (London, 1965); *The Happy Time*, 1968; *Sugar*, 1972. Director — *My Mother, My Father And Me*, 1963; *I Do! I Do!*, 1966; *Irene*, 1973; *Mack And Mabel*, 1974; *Rockabye Hamlet*, 1976; *The Act* 1977.
Also: began as a dancer in supper clubs ("Gower and Jeanne," "Gower and Bell"); various dance roles in films; television and nightclub appearances.
Awards: Tony Awards — *Bye Bye Birdie, Hello Dolly, The Happy Time;* (Choreography

and Direction); Tony and Donaldson Awards — *Lend An Ear* (Choreography).

HAROLD CLURMAN, *Director/Critic*
Born: September 18, 1901; New York, New York
Broadway (Director): numerous productions including *The Member Of The Wedding*, 1950; *Desire Under The Elms*, 1952; *The Time Of The Cuckoo*, 1952; *The Ladies Of The Corridor*, 1953; *Mlle. Colombe*, 1954; *Bus Stop*, 1955; *Tiger At The Gates*, 1955; *Pipe Dream*, 1955; *Waltz Of The Toreadors*, 1957; *Orpheus Descending*, 1957; *A Touch Of The Poet*, 1958; *Heartbreak House*, 1959; *A Shot In The Dark*, 1961; *Incident At Vichy*, 1964. Also co-produced *Truckline Cafe*, 1946 and *All My Sons*, 1947.
Theatre Companies: The Group Theatre — Co-Founder and Executive Director, 1937-41; directed *Awake And Sing, Paradise Lost, Golden Boy, Rocket To The Moon, The Gentle People, Night Music* and *Retreat To Pleasure.* Mark Taper Forum — directed *Uncle Vanya*, 1969. Repertory Theatre Of Lincoln Center — Executive Consultant, 1963.
Critic: The New Republic, 1949-53; The London Observer, Guest Critic, 1959-63; The Nation, since 1953.
Author: *The Fervent Years, On Directing, Lies Like Truth.*
Awards: George Jean Nathan Award — *Lies Like Truth;* Donaldson Award — *The Member Of The Wedding* (director); Chevalier Of The French Legion Of Honor.

ALEXANDER H. COHEN, *Producer*
Born: July 24, 1920; New York, New York
Broadway: numerous productions including *Angel Street*, 1941; *Of "V" We Sing*, 1942; *Make A Wish*, 1951; *At The Drop Af A Hat*, 1959; *An Evening With Nichols And May*, 1960; *An Evening With Yves Montand*, 1961; *Beyond The Fringe* (also 1964, 1965); *The School For Scandal*, 1963; *The Ages Of Man*, 1963; *Man And Bay*, 1963; *An Evening With Maurice Chevalier*, 1963; *Hamlet*, 1964; *Baker Street*, 1965; *The Devils*, 1965; *A Time For Singing*, 1966; *Ivanov*, 1966; *Halfway Up The Tree*, 1967; *Marlene Dietrich*, 1967; *Black Comedy*, 1967; *The Unknown Soldier And His Wife*, 1967; *The Homecoming*, 1967; *Little Murders*, 1967; *Dear World*, 1969; *Home*, 1970; *Good Evening*, 1973; *Ulysses In Nighttown*, 1974; *Who's Who In Hell*, 1974;

We Interrupt This Program, 1975; *Comedians*, 1976; *Hellzapoppin*, 1976; *Anna Christie*, 1977, *I Remember Mama*, 1979.

Also: over fifteen productions in London including *Halfway Up The Tree, Man And Boy, The Merchant Of Venice, Harvey, The Price, Plaza Suite, Applause and Comedians;* producer of the annual Tony Awards for television.

Awards: Tony Awards — *The Homecoming;* New York Critics Award — *Home.*

BETTY COMDEN, *Playright/Lyricist/Actor*
Born: May 3, 1919; Brooklyn, New York

Co-Lyricist and Co-Author (with Adolph Green): *On The Town,* 1944; *Billion Dollar Baby,* 1945; *Two On The Aisle,* 1951; *Wonderful Town,* 1953; *Peter Pan,* 1954; *Bells Are Ringing,* 1956; *Say, Darling,* 1958; *Do Re Mi (co-lyricist), 1960; Subways Are For Sleping,* 1961; *Fade-Out, Fade-In,* 1964; *Hallelujah, Baby!* (co-lyricist), 1967; *Applause* (co-author), 1970; *Lorelei* (co-lyricist), 1974; *The Twentieth Century,* 1978.

Also: appeared in *On The Town,* 1944 and *A Party With Betty Comden And Adolph Green* (1958): collaborated with Adolph Green on various screenplays including *On The Town, Singing In The Rain, It's Always Fair Weather, Auntie Mame* and *Bells Are Ringing.*

Awards: Tony Awards — *Wonderful Town, Hallelujah Baby!, Applause;* Obie Award — *A Party With Betty Comden And Adolph Green;* Donaldson Award — *Wonderful Town.*

FRANK CORSARO, *Director*
Born: December 22, 1924; New York, New York

Off-Broadway: *No Exit,* 1947; *Family Reunion,* 1947; *Creditors,* 1949; *Heartbreak House,* 1950; *Naked,* 1950, *The Scarecrow,* 1953.

Broadway: *The Honeys,* 1955; *A Hatful Of Rain,* 1955; *The Night Circus,* 1958; *The Night Of The Iguana,* 1961; *Baby Want A Kiss,* 1964; *Treemonisha,* 1975; *Cold Storage,* 1977; *Knockout,* 1979.

Other: *The Taming Of The Shrew* (NY City Center), 1951; four productions at Rooftop Theatre, Atlanta, 1951; three productions (including world premiere of *Night Of The Iguana)* at the Spoleto Festival, 1959; world premiere (London) *Oh Dad, Poor Dad ...,* 1961.

Also: director of numerous productions for the New York City Opera; directed various operas in Seattle, St. Paul, Houston, Atlanta and Washington, D.C.

HUME CRONYN, *Actor/Director*
Born: July 18, 1911; London, Ontario, Canada

Theatre Companies: Montreal Repertory Theatre — various productions, 1930-31. Barter Theatre Company — actor/director, 1934. Jitney Players — tour, 1935. Group Theatre — *Retreat To Pleasure,* 1940. Actor's Laboratory Theatre — *The Male Animal, Portrait Of A Madonna* (director), 1946. Lakewood Theatre — various productions, 1939-40. ANTA — *Hamlet* (tour), 1949. Phoenix Theatre — founding member; *Madam, Will You Walk* (also director), 1953. Guthrie Theatre — 1963 (First) season, 1965 season. Mark Taper Forum — *The Miser,* 1968. Stratford National Theatre Company — *Hadrian VII,* 1969. Repertory Theatre Of Lincoln Center — Samuel Beckett Festival, 1972. Stratford (Ontario) Shakespeare Festival — 1976-77 season. Long Wharf Theatre — *The Gin Game* (also Broadway), 1977.

Broadway: *Hipper's Holiday,* 1934; *Boy Meets Girl,* 1935; *High Tor,* 1937; *Room Service,* 1937; *There's Always A Breeze,* 1938, *Escape This Night,* 1938; *Off To Buffalo,* 1939; *The Three Sisters,* 1939; *The Weak Link,* 1940; *Mr. Big,* 1941; *The Survivors,* 1948; *The Fourposter,* 1951; *The Honeys,* 1955; *A Day By The Sea,* 1955; *The Man In The Dog Suit,* 1957; *Triple Play* (also director), 1959; *Big Fish, Little Fish,* 1961; *Hamlet,* 1964; *The Physicists,* 1964; *A Delicate Balance,* 1966; *Promenada All,* 1972; *In Two Keys.* 1974.

Director: *Now I Lay Me Down To Sleep,* 1950; *Hilda Crane,* 1950; *The Egg Head,* 1957; *Promenada All* (tour), 1972.

Also: Producer, *USO tours,* 1942; Producer, *Slow Dance On The Killing Ground* (Broadway), 1964; appeared in *The Caine Mutiny Court Martial* (Ahmanson Theatre, LA), 1971; numerous films include *The Seventh Cross Lifeboat, The Postman Always Rings Twice, Sunrise At Campobello, There Was A Crooked Man, Parallax View.*

Awards: Tony Awards — *Hamlet;* Obie Award — *Krapp's Last Tape* (Beckett Festival).

JOHN CULLUM, *Actor*
Born: March 2, 1930; Knoxville, Tennessee

Broadway: *Camelot,* 1960; *Hamlet,* 1964; *On A Clear Day You Can See Forever,* 1965; *Man Of La Mancha,* 1967; *1776,* 1970; *Vivat! Vivat! Regina,* 1972; *Shenandoah,* 1975; *Kings,* 1976; *The Trip Back Down,* 1977; *On The Twentieth Century,* 1978.

Off-Broadway: *Saving Grace,* 1963; *Thistle In My Bed,* 1963; *Three Hand Reel,* 1966; *The Elizabethans,* 1972.

Theatre Companies: *Engaged, Or Cheviot's Choice* (Goodspeed Opera House), 1966; *The Lady's Not For Burning* (Goodman Memorial Theatre), 1973; *The School For Wives* (Phoenix Theatre), 1971; *El Captain* (Folger Theatre), 1974; *Carnival Dreams* (New Dramatists), 1978.

Also: *As You Like It* (musical, White Barn Theatre, Westport), 1964; *Camelot* (Papermill Playhouse), 1964; *The King And I,* 1972 and *Carousel,* 1973 (Jones Beach Theatre); *The Archbishop's Ceiling* (Kennedy Center), 1977.

Director: *Red, Blue, Green* (Goodspeed Opera House), 1978; *Zinnia* (Colonades Theatre Lab), 1977; *People In Show Business Make Long Goodbyes* (Off-Broadway), 1979.

Awards: Tony Awards — *Shenandoah, On The Twentieth Century;* Drama Desk Award — *Shenandoah.*

GORDON DAVIDSON, *Producer/Director*
Born: May 7, 1934; Brooklyn, New York

Producer: *Borak* (co-producer; Off-Broadway), 1960; Theatre Group, University Of California (Los Angeles), Managing Director, 1964-66; Mark Taper Forum, Artistic Director since 1966.

Director: Theatre Group, University Of California — *The Deputy,* 1965; *Candide,* 1966. Mark Taper Forum — various productions including *The Devils,* 1967; *Who's Happy Now?,* 1967; *In The Matter Of J. Robert Oppenheimer,* 1968; *Murderous Angels,* 1970; *Rosebloom,* 1970; *Trial Of The Catonsville Nine* (also Off-Broadway and Broadway), 1971; *Henry IV,* Part 1, 1972; *Bernstein's Mass,* 1973 (also Kennedy Center, 1971); *Hamlet,* 1974; *Savages,* 1974 (also Hudson Guild Theatre, 1977); *The Shadow Box,* 1975 (also *Long Wharf Theatre and Broadway, 1977); And Where She Stops Nobody Knows,* 1976; *Black Angel,* 1978.

Awards — Tony Award — *The Shadow Box;* Margo Jones Award — *1970;* Obie Award —

The Trial Of The Catonsville Nine; Los Angeles Drama Critics Award — *Savages.*

ALFRED DE LIAGRE, JR., *Producer/Director*
Born: October 6, 1904; Passaic, New Jersey

Producer/Director: *Yes, My Darling Daughter,* 1937; *I Am My Youth,* 1937; *Mr. and Mrs. North,* 1941; *The Walrus And The Carpenter,* 1941; *Ask My Friend Sandy,* 1943; *The Madwoman of Chaillot,* 1948 (London, 1951); *Second Threshold,* 1951; *Nature's Way,* 1957.

Co-Producer/Director: *Three Cornered Moon,* 1933; *By Your Leave,* 1934; *Pure In Heart,* 1934; *Petticoat Fever,* 1935; *Fresh Fields,* 1936; *The Deep Blue Sea,* 1952; *Escapade,* 1952; *The Golden Apple,* 1954; *The Tumbler,* 1960.

Producer: *The Voice of The Turtle,* 1943 (London, 1951); *The Druid Castle,* 1947; *Janus,* 1955 (London, 1957); *The Girls In 509,* 1958; *J.B.,* 1958; *Kwamina,* 1961; *The Irregular Verb To Love,* 1963; *Photo Finish,* 1963; *Deathtrap,* 1978.

Also: Board of Directors — League of New York Theatres, American Theatre Wing, ANTA, American Shakespeare Theatre.

Awards: Tony Award and Pulitzer Prize — *J.B.;* NY Drama Critics Awards — *The Madwoman of Chaillot, The Golden Apple.*

COLLEEN DEWHURST, *Actor*
Born: June 3, 1929; Montreal, Canada

Theatre Companies: New York Shakespeare Festival — *The Taming Of The Shrew,* 1956; *Titus Andronicus,* 1956; *MacBeth,* 1957; *Antony And Cleopatra,* 1959, 1963; *Hamlet,* 1972; *Taken In Marriage,* 1979. Circle In The Square — *Children Of Darkness,* 1958; *Desire Under The Elms,* 1963; *Mourning Becomes Electra,* 1972. Buffalo Studio Arena — *A Moon For The Misbegotten,* 1965; *The Little Foxes,* 1966. Repertory Theatre of Lincoln Center — *Good Woman of Setzuan,* 1970. Mark Taper Forum — *A Moon For The Misbegotten,* 1975. Long Wharf Theatre — *Artichoke,* 1975.

Broadway: *Tamburlaine The Great,* 1956; *The Country Wife,* 1957; *All The Way Home,* 1960; *Great Day In The Morning,* 1962; *Ballad Of The Sad Cafe,* 1963; *More Stately Mansions,* 1967; *All Over,* 1971; *A Moon For The Misbegotten,* 1973; *Who's Afraid Of Vir-*

ginia Woolf, 1976; *An Almost Perfect Person*, 1977.

Off-Broadway: *The Eagle Has Two Heads*, 1956; *Camille*, 1956; *Caligula*, 1960; *Hello And Goodbye*, 1969.

Also: various films including *The Nun's Story*, *A Fine Madness* and *Annie Hall*; numerous television appearances.

Awards: Tony Awards—*All The Way Home*, *A Moon For The Misbegotten*; Drama Desk Awards — *Hello And Goodbye*, *All Over*, *A Moon For The Misbegotten*; Obie Awards — *The Eagle Has Two Heads*, *The Taming Of The Shrew*, *Desire Under The Elms*.

FRED EBB, *Lyricist*
Born: April 8, 1932; New York, New York

With John Kander as Composer: *Flora, The Red Menace*, 1965; *Cabaret*, 1966; *The Happy Time*, 1968; *Zorba*, 1968; *70 Girls 70* (also co-author), 1971; *Chicago*, 1975; *2 x 5*, 1976; *The Act*, 1978.

Also: books and lyrics for *Morning Sun* (Phoenix), 1963; wrote sketches for *That Was The Week That Was* on television and material for various nightclub performers.

Awards: Tony Award—*Cabaret*.

PETER EVANS, *Actor*
Born: May 27, 1950; Englewood, New Jersey

Theatre Companies: Williamstown Theatre Festival — various productions during 1972, 1973, 1975, 1977 and 1978 seasons including *Six Characters In Search Of An Author*, *Design For Living* and *A Month In The Country*; founding member, 1972, Williamstown Second Company, appeared in *Measure For Measure* and *Peer Gynt*. Manhattan Theatre Club — *Life Class*, 1975; *Don Juan Comes Back From The War*, 1979. Long Wharf Theatre and New York Shakespeare Festival —*Streamers*, 1976.

Off-Broadway: *A Life In The Theatre*, 1977.

Awards: Clarence Derwent Award—*Streamers*.

TOVAH FELDSHUH, *Actor*
Born: December 27; New York, New York

Theatre Companies: Guthrie Theatre — twenty productions during 1971-72 and 1972-73 seasons. Springfield Stage/West — 1973-74 season. Chelsea Theatre Center — *Yentl* (also Broadway), 1974. Amercian Place Theatre — *Straws In The Wind*, 1975.

American Shakespeare Festival—*As You Like It*, *The Crucible*, 1976. Brooklyn Academy Of Music — *The Three Sisters*, 1977. McCarter Theatre—*The Torchbearers*, 1978.

Broadway: *Cyrano*, 1973; *Dreyfus In Rehearsal*, 1974; *Rodgers And Hart*, 1975; *Sarava*, 1979.

Also: various television appearances including *Holocaust*.

Awards: Obie and Drama Desk Awards — *Yentl*.

JOSE FERRER, *Actor/Director/Producer*
Born: January 8, 1912; Santurce, Puerto Rico

Actor: *A Slight Case Of Murder*, 1935; *Spring Dance*, 1936; *Brother Rat*, 1936; *In Clover*, 1937; *How To Get Tough About It*, 1938; *Missouri Legend*, 1938; *Mamba's Daughters*, 1939; *Key Largo*, 1939; *Charley's Aunt*, 1940; *Vickie*, 1942; *Let's Face It*, 1942; *Othello*, 1943; *Cyrano de Bergerac*, 1946; *Volpone, Angel Street, Four One Act Comedies* By Chekhov, *The Alchemist, S.S. Glencairn* and *The Insect Comedy* (New York City Theatre Company), 1948; *The Silver Whistle*, 1948; *Twentieth Century*, 1950; *The Strike*, 1952; *Richard III*, 1953; *Charley's Aunt*, 1953; *Cyrano de Bergerac*, 1953; *Edwin Booth*, 1958; *The Girl Who Came To Supper*, 1963; *Man Of La Mancha*, 1965; *Long Day's Journey Into Night*, 1977; *A Life In The Theatre*, 1978. Various other appearances on tour and in stock.

Director: *Vickie*, 1962; *Strange Fruit* (also producer), 1945; *A Tragedian In Spite Of Himself* and *The Wedding* (Chekhov One Acts), *S.S. Glencairn* and *The Insect Comedy*, 1948; *Twentieth Century*, 1950; *Stalag 17* (also producer), 1951; *The Four poster*, 1951; *The Shrike* (also producer), 1952; *The Chase* (also producer), 1952; *My Third Angels*, 1953; *Charley's Aunt*, 1953; *Cyrano de Bergerac*, 1953; *The Fourposter*, 1955; *Oh, Captain* (also co-author), 1958; *Edwin Booth* (also producer), 1958; *The Andersonville Trial*, 1959; *The Web And The Rock*, 1972; *Great Director*, Cleveland Playhouse, 1972; *A Yard Of Sun*, 1972; *Cyrano de Bergerac* (Chichester Festival), 1975;

Also: film appearances include *Cyrano de Bergerac, Moulin Rouge, The Caine Mutiny, The Shrike* (also director), *Lawrence Of Arabia, Ship Of Fools, Enter Laughing*; numerous television appearances.

Awards: Tony Awards—*Cyrano de Bergerac*

and *The Shrike* (actor), *Stalag 17*, *The Shrike*, *The Fourposter* (director); Donaldson Awards — *Othello*, *The Shrike* (director, actor); Academy (Oscar) Award — *Cyrano de Bergerac*.

JULES FISHER, *Lighting Designer*
Born: November 12, 1937; Norristown, Pennsylvania

Broadway: numerous productions including *Most Happy Fella*, 1956; *Ziegfield Follies*, 1956; *Mr. Wonderful*, 1956; *Spoon River Anthology*, 1963; *Anyone Can Whistle*, 1964; *High Spirits*, 1964; *The Subject Was Roses*, 1964; *Half A Sixpence*, 1965; *Illya, Darling*, 1967; *Little Murders*, 1967; *You Know I Can't Hear You When The Water's Running*, 1967; *Hair*, 1968; *Butterflies Are Free*, 1969; *Jesus Christ Superstar*, 1971; *Lanny*, 1971; *No, No Nanette*, 1971; *Pippin*, 1972; *Seasaw*, 1973; *Billy*, 1974; *Liza*, 1974; *Ulysses In Nighttown*, 1974; *Thieves*, 1974; *Chicago*, 1975; *Beatlemania*, 1977; *American Buffalo*, 1977; *Dancin'*, 1978.

Co-Producer: *Lenny*, 1971; *Dancin'*, 1978.

Also: Lighting designer for many Off-Broadway productions including *Sergeant Musgrave's Dance*, 1966; *Scuba Duba*, 1967; *You're A Good Man, Charlie Brown*, 1967; *Steambath*, 1970; various productions for New York City Center and Circle In The Square.

Awards: Tony Awards — *Pippin*, *Ulysses In Nighttown*, *Dancin'*.

HENRY FONDA, *Actor*
Born: May 10, 1905; Grand Island, Nebraska

Broadway: *The Game Of Love And Death*, 1929; *The Farmer Takes A Wife*, 1934; *Blow Ye Winds*, 1937; *Mister Roberts*, 1948; *Point Of No Return*, 1951; *Caine Mutiny Court Martial*, 1954; *Two For The Seesaw*, 1958; *Silent Night, Lonely Night*, 1959; *Critics Choice*, 1960; *A Gift Of Time*, 1962; *Generation*, 1965; *Our Town*, 1969; *The Trial Of A. Lincoln*, 1974; *Clarence Darrow*, 1974; *First Monday In October*, 1978.

Tours: *Mister Roberts*, 1951; *Point Of No Return*, 1952; *Fathers Against Sons Against Fathers*, 1970; *The Caine Mutiny Court Martial*, 1971; *The Trial Of A. Lincoln*, 1974; *Clarence Darrow*, 1975.

Also: over seventy films including *Jezebel*, *Jesse James*, *Young Mr. Lincoln*, *Drums Along The Mohawk*, *The Grapes Of Wrath*, *The Ox Bow Incident*, *Daisy Kenyon*, *Mister Roberts*, *War and Peace*, *Twelve Angry Men*, *Advise And Consent*, *The Best Man*.

Awards: Tony Award — *Mister Roberts*; Drama Desk Award—*Clarence Darrow*.

RICHARD FOREMAN,
Author/Director/Designer
Born: June 10, 1937; New York, New York

Ontological-Hysteric Theatre: Founder/Director since 1968; Author/Director/Designer *Angleface*, 1968; *Total Recall* (Sophia-Wisdom: Part Two), 1970; *Hcohtienla On Hotel China; Parts 1 & 2*, 1971; *Evidence*, 1972; *Sophia-Wisdom: Part 3: The Cliffs*, 1973; *Particle Theory*, 1973; *Pain (t) and Vertical Mobility*, 1974; *Pandering To The Masses: A Misrepresentation*, 1975; *Rhoda In Potatoland*, 1975; *Livre Des Splendeurs*, 1976; *Book Of Splendors: Part II (Book Of Levers) Action At A Distance*, 1977; *Blvd. De Paris: I've Got The Shakes*, 1977; also *City Archives* (video play), 1977; *Strong Medicine* (feature film), 1978.

Music-Theatre Pieces: Author/Director/Designer *Elephant Steps* (Berkshire Music Festival), 1968 and Hunter College Opera Theatre, 1970), *Dream Tantras For Western Massachusetts* (Lenox Arts Centre), 1971; *Dr. Selavy's Magic Theatre* (Lenox Arts Center and Off-Broadway), 1972; *Hotel For Criminals* (Lenox Arts Center, 1974 and Off-Broadway, 1975); *The American Imagination* (Music Theatre Performing Group), 1978.

Also: Author/Director/Designer, *Ida-Eyed* (New Dramatists), 1969; *Real Magic In New York* (concert production), 1970; *Classical Therapy Or A Week Under The Influence* (Festival d'Automne, Paris), 1973; directed *Threepenny Opera* (New York Shakespeare Festival at Lincoln Center), 1976.

Awards: Obie Awards—*Elephant Steps* (Author/Director), *Rhoda In Potatoland* (Author), Director Ontological-Hysteric Theatre.

BOB FOSSE, *Director/Choreographer*
Born: June 23, 1927; Chicago, Illinois

Choreographer: *Pajama Game*, 1954; *Damn Yankees*, 1955; *Bells Are Ringing* (Co-Choreographer), 1956; *New Girl In Town*, 1957; *How To Succeed In Business Without Really Trying*, 1961.

Director/Choreographer: *Redhead*, 1959; *Little Me* (Co-Director), 1962; *Pippin*, 1972;

Liza, 1974; *Chicago* (also Co-Author), 1975; *Dancin'*, 1978.
Also: directed the films *Sweet Charity, Lenny, Cabaret* and the television special, *Liza With A Z.*
Awards: Tony Awards — *Pajama Game, Damn Yankees, Redhead, Little Me, Sweet Charity, Pippin, Dancin'* (for choreography); *Pippin* (for direction). Drama Desk Award (direction and choreography) — *Pippin.* Donaldson Award—*Pajama Game.* Academy (Oscar) Award—*Cabaret.*

JACK GILFORD, *Actor*
Born: July 25, 1907; New York City
Broadway: *Meet The People*, 1940; *They Should Have Stood In Bed*, 1942; *Count Me In*, 1942; *Alic And Kicking*, 1950; *The Diary Of Anne Frank*, 1955; *Romanoff and Juliet*, 1957; *Drink To Me Only*, 1958; *Look After Lulu*, 1959; *The Tenth Man*, 1959; *A Funny Thing Happened On The Way To The Forum*, 1962; *Cabaret*, 1966; *Three Men On A Horse*, 1969; *No, No Nanette*, 1971; *The Sunshine Boys*, 1972; *Sly Fox*, 1976;
Off-Broadway: *The World of Shalom Aleichem*, 1953; *Passion Of Gross*, 1955; *Once Upon A Mattress*, 1959; *The Policeman*, 1961.
Also: early career in vaudeville; five seasons at the Metropolitan Opera House in *Die Fledermaus;* various film, television, radio and night club appearances.

ANITA GILLETTE, *Actor*
Born: August 16, 1938; Baltimore, Maryland
Broadway: *Gypsy*, 1959; *Carnival*, 1961; *All American*, 1962; *Mr. President*, 1962; *Kelly*, 1965; *Don't Drink The Water*, 1966; *Cabaret*, 1966; *Jimmy*, 1969; *Chapter Two*, 1977.
Theatre Companies: *Rich And Famous* (New York Shakespeare Festival), 1976; *The Importance Of Being Earnest* and *Travesties* (Mark Taper Forum), 1977.
Also: *Sketchbook* (Off-Broadway), 1960; *Guys And Dolls* (Canada, 1962 and NY City Center, 1965); *Pocahontas* (London), 1963; *The Great Waltz* (LA Music Center), 1965; *Knickerbocker Holiday* (LA Civic Light Opera), 1971; *South Pacific* (Petersburgh Light Opera), 1974; various television appearances.

MILTON GOLDMAN, *Agent*
Born: August 12, 1914;
New Brunswick, New Jersey

Agencies: started in the employ of A.S. Lyons, 1947; later joined the *Paul Small Agency;* formed the *Milton Goldman Agency,* 1954, which became part of *Ashley-Steiner,* 1957, which evolved into Internation Creative Management, where Mr. Goldman is presently head of the Theatre Department and Vice-President.
Clients: present and former include *Tallulah Bankhead, Faye Dunaway, John Gielgud, Jack Gilford, Hermione Gingold, Cedric Hardwicke, Eileen Heckart, Charlton Heston, Grace Kelly, Jack Lemmon, Lee Marvin, Walter Matthau, Ethel Merman, Laurence Olivier, Maureen O'Sullivan, Anthony Quayle, Lynn Redgrave, Ralph Richardson, Cyril Ritchard, Eva Marie Saint, Maureen Stapleton.*

MORTON GOTTLIEB, *Producer*
Born: May 2, 1921; Brooklyn, New York
Broadway (Co-Producer): *His And Hers*, 1954; *Enter Laughing*, 1963 (Producer); *Chips With Everything*, 1963; *The White House*, 1964; *P.S. I Love You*, 1964; *The Killing Of Sister George*, 1966; *Come Live With Me*, 1967; *The Promise*, 1967; *Lovers*, 1968; *We Bombed In New Haven*, 1968; *The Munday Scheme*, 1969; *Sleuth*, 1970; *Veronica's Room*, 1973; *Same Time Next Year*, 1975; *Tribute*, 1978; *The Faith Healer*, 1979.
Also: Company or General Manager for numerous Broadway productions; General Manager, *American Shakespeare Festival* 1956, 1957; producer of the film, *Sleuth.*
Awards: Tony Award—*Sleuth.*

ADOLPH GREEN, *Playwright/Lyricist/ Actor*
Born: Bronx, New York
Co-Lyricist and Co-Author *(with Betty Comden):* On *The Town*, 1944; *Billion Dollar Baby*, 1945; *Two On The Aisle*, 1951; *Wonderful Town*, 1953; *Peter Pan*, 1954; *Bells Are Ringing*, 1956; *Say, Darling*, 1958; *Do Re Mi* (co-lyricist), 1960; *Subways Are For Sleeping*, 1961; *Fade-Out, Fade-In*, 1964; *Hallelujah, Baby!* (co-lyricist), 1967; *Applause* (co-author), 1970; *Lorelei* (co-lyricist), 1974.
Also: appeared in *On The Town* (1944) and *A Party With Betty Comden And Adolph Green* (1958); collaborated with Betty Comden on various screenplays including *On The Town, Singing In The Rain, It's Always Fair Weather, Auntie Mame* and *Bells Are Ringing.*
Awards: Tony Awards — *Wonderful Town,*

Hallulujah Baby!, Applause; Obie Award — *A Party With Betty Comden And Adolph Green;* Donaldson Award — *Wonderful Town.*

JOEL GREY, *Actor*
Born: April 11, 1932; Cleveland, Ohio
Broadway: *Come Blow Your Horn,* 1961; *Half A Sixpence,* 1965; *Cabaret,* 1968; *George M,* 1967; *Goodtime Charley,* 1975; *The Grand Tour,* 1978.
Theatre Companies: *The Littlest Revue* (Phoenix Theatre), 1956; *Harry, Noon and Night* (American Place Theatre), 1065; *Marco Polo Sings A Solo* (New York Shakespeare Festival), 1976.
Also: *Stop The World, I Want To Get Off* (National Company), 1963-64; films include *Buffalo Bill And The Indians, The Seven Percent Solution, Cabaret;* Various television appearances.
Awards: Tony Award — *Cabaret,* Academy (Oscar) Award — *Cabaret.*

TAMMY GRIMES, *Actor*
Born: January 30, 1934; Lynn, Massachusetts
Theatre Companies: *The Littlest Revue* (Phoenix), 1956; *Henry IV, Part I* and *The Winter's Tale* (Stratford Ontario Shakespeare Festival), 1958; *The Imaginary Invalid,* 1971 and *The Taming Of The Shrew,* 1973 (Philadelphia Drama Guild); *Gabrielle* (Buffalo Studio Arena), 1975; *Tartuffe* (Circle In The Square), 1977.
Broadway: *Bus Stop,* 1956; *Look After Lulu,* 1959; *The Unsinkable Molly Brown,* 1960; *Rattle Of A Simple Man,* 1962; *High Spirits,* 1964; *The Only Game In Town,* 1968; *Private Lives,* 1969; *A Musical Jubilee,* 1975; *California Suite,* 1976.
Also: *Clerembard* (Off-Broadway), 1957; *The Cradle Will Rock* (City Center), 1960; *The Private Ear And The Public Eye* (tour), 1965; numerous television appearances in variety and dramatic specials.
Awards: Tony Awards — *The Unsinkable Molly Brown, Private Lives.*

JOHN GUARE, *Playwright*
Born: February 5, 1938; New York, New York
Theatre Companies: *Did You Write My Name In The Snow* (Yale University), 1962; *To Tony Pantoni, We Leave A Credenza* (New Dramatists), 1964; *The Loveliest Afternoon Of The Year, Something I'll Tell You Tuesday* (Cafe Cino), 1966; *Muzeeka* (Mark Taper Forum, also Off-Broadway), 1967. New York Shakespeare Festival — *Two Gentlemen Of Verona* (lyrics and co-adaptor), *Central Park and Broadway,* 1971; *Marco Polo Sings A Solo* (also at Cyrus Pierce Theatre, Nantucket, 1973), 1976; *Rich And Famous,* 1976; *Landscape Of The Body* (also at Goodman Memorial Theatre), 1977.
Also: *The House Of Blue Leaves* (Off-Broadway), 1971; *A Day For Surprises* (London), 1971.
Broadway: *Cop Out,* 1969; *Home Fires,* 1969; *Bosoms And Neglect* (also at Goodman Memorial Theatre), 1979.
Awards: Tony Award — *Two Gentlemen Of Verona;* New York Critics Award — *The House Of Blue Leaves, Two Gentlemen Of Verona;* Obie Awards — *Museeka, The House of Blue Leaves;* Drama Desk Award — *Two Gentlemen Of Verona.*

MARGOT HARLEY, *Actor/Producer*
Born: November 21, 1935
The Acting Company: Co-Founder, 1972 and Executive Director; also administrator of The Drama Division of the Juilliard School since 1969; Co-Producer, *The Robber Bridegroom* (Broadway), 1976.
Actor/Dancer: member Doris Humphrey Repertory Dance Company, 1955-57; appeared Off-Broadway in *The Boy Friend,* 1958; *The Crystal Heart,* 1960; *Ernest In Love,* 1960; appeared on Broadway in *Milk And Honey,* 1961.
Also: Associate Producer KQED, 1965-67; Executive Director, *Friends Of Channel 13,* 1967-69.

JULIE HARRIS, *Actor*
Born: December 2, 1925;
    Grosse Point, Michigan
Broadway: *It's A Gift,* 1945; *The Playboy Of The Western World,* 1946; *Alice In Wonderland,* 1947; *Macbeth,* 1948; *Sundown Beach,* 1948; *The Young And The Fair,* 1948; *Magnolia Alley,* 1949; *Monserrat,* 1949; *The Member Of The Wedding,* 1950; *I Am A Camera,* 1951; *Mlle. Colombe,* 1954; *The Lark,* 1955; *Country Wife,* 1957; *Warm Peninsula,* 1959; *Little Moon Of Alban,* 1960; *A Shot In The Dark,* 1961; *Marathon '33,* 1963; *Skyscraper,* 1963; *Ready When You Are, C.B.,* 1964; *Forty Carats,* 1968; *And Miss Reardon Drinks A Little,* 1971; *Voices,* 1972; *The Last Of Mrs. Lincoln,* 1972; *In Praise Of*

Love, 1974; *The Belle Of Amherst,* 1977.

Theatre Companies: New York Shakespeare Festival—*Hamlet* (Central Park), 1964; *The Au Pair Man* (Lincoln Center), 1973. Stratford (Ontario) Shakespeare Festival — *Romeo And Juliet, King John,* 1960. Repertory Theatre Of New Orleans — *The Women,* 1970.

Also: various films (including *The Member Of The Wedding, I Am A Camera* and *East Of Eden*) and television (including *Wind From The South, Little Moon Of Alban* and *Victoria Regina*) appearances.

Awards: Tony Awards—*I Am A Camera, The Lark, Forty Carats, The Last Of Mrs. Lincoln, The Belle Of Amherst;* Donaldson Awards — *The Member Of The Wedding, I Am A Camera;* Drama Desk Awards — *The Member Of The Wedding, The Last Of Mrs. Lincoln.*

AL HIRSCHFELD, *Theatre Caricaturist*
Born: June 21, 1903

Theater caricaturist for the New York Times since 1925

Permanent Collections: St. Louis Art Museum, Butler Institute Of American Art, Fogg Museum, Cleveland Art Museum, Whitney Art Museum, Metropolitan Museum Of Art, Brooklyn Museum, Museum Of Modern Art, Hyde Park Museum, Davenport Museum, Magnes Museum.

Published Works: Manhattan Oases, Harlem, Show Business Is No Business, The American Theatre, The World Of Hirschfeld, The Lively Years (in collaboration with Brooks Atkinson).

GEOFFREY HOLDER, *Dancer/Designer/Choreographer/Director*
Born: August 1, 1930; Port-of-Spain, Trinidad

Broadway: *House Of Flowers* (dancer), 1954; *Waiting For Godot* (actor), 1957; *Josephine Baker's Revue* (dancer), 1964; *The Wiz* (director/costume designer), 1975; *Timbuktu* (director/costume designer), 1978.

Choreographer: *Brouhaha* (Folksbiene Playhouse), 1960; *Mhil Dalim* (Actors Studio), 1964; *I Got A Song* (Buffalo Studio Arena), 1974.

Also: appeared in the Actors' Studio productions of *The Mark Of St. George And The Dragon,* 1973 and *From The Memory Of Pontius Pilate,* 1976; appeared as a dancer in *Aida* and *La Perichole* (Metorpolitan Opera), 1956-57; *Showboat* (Jones Beach Theatre),

1957 and with the Geoffrey Holder Dance Company (Kaufmann Auditorium, 1956-60 and Harkness Dance Festival, 1963); choreographed and designed costumes for *Three Songs For One* (Jacob's Pillow Dance Festival), 1964, Harkness Dance Festival, 1966 and Dance Theatre of Harlem; author of *Black Gods, Green Islands* and *The Geoffrey Holder Caribbean Cookbook;* various film, television and nightclub appearances.

Awards: Tony and Drama Desk Awards — *The Wiz*

ISRAEL HOROVITZ, *Playwright*
Born: March 31, 1939;
        Wakefield, Massachusetts

Early Plays: *The Comeback,* 1958; *The Death Of Bernard The Believer,* 1960; *This Play Is Me,* 1961; *The Hanging Of Emanuel,* 1962; *Hop,* 1963; *Skip,* 1964; *Jump,* 1964; *Brownstone,* 1967.

Off-Broadway: *It's Called The Sugar Plum* and *The Indian Wants The Bronx,* 1968; *Leader* and *The Honest To God Schnozzola,* 1969; *Line and Acrobats,* 1971; *The Primary English Class,* 1976.

Theatre Companies: *Rats* (Cafe Au Go Go), 1968; *Morning* (Spoleto Festival, later presented as *Chiaroscuro*), 1968; *Dr. Hero* (Actor's Company, Great Neck and The Shade Company, NYC), 1972; *Shooting Gallery* (WPA Theatre), 1972; *Alfred The Great* (Pittsburgh Playhouse), 1973; *Spared* (Manhattan Theatre Club), 1974; *Turnstile* (Dartmouth College and The Cubiculo), 1974; *Our Father's Failing* (Goodman Theatre), 1975; *Dr. Hero* (Cubiculo), 1976; *The Wakefield Plays* (New Dramatists), 1976; *The Reason We Eat* (Hartman Theatre Company), 1977; *Quannapowitt Quartet* (New York Shakespeare Festival) 1978-79.

Also: author of several screenplays and the novel, *Cappella*

Awards: Obie Awards—*It's Called The Sugar Plum* and *The Indian Wants The Bronx, Leader* and *The Honest To God Schnozzola;* Vernon Rice-Drama Desk Award—*It's Called the Sugar Plum* and *The Indian Wants The Bronx;* American Academy Of Arts And Letters Award in Literature.

JOHN HOUSEMAN, *Producer/Director/Actor*
Born: September 22, 1902;
        Bucharest, Rumania

Theatre Companies: Federal Theatre (WPA) Project — managing producer, Negro Theatre and Classical Theatre Projects, 1936-37. Co-Founder Mercury Theatre which produced — *Julius Caesar*, 1937; *Shoemaker's Holiday*, 1938; *Heartbreak House*, *1938*; *The Cradle Will Rock*, 1938; *Danton's Death*, 1938. American Shakespeare Theatre — Artistic Director, 1956-59; directed *Othello*, *Hamlet*, *All's Well That Ends Well*; co-directed five other productions and *Murder In The Cathedral*, 1966; *Macbeth*, 1967;. Theatre Group Of The University Of California (Los Angeles) — Artistic Director, 1959-64; directed various productions. Phoenix theatre — directed *Coriolanus*, 1959. A.P.A. — Producing Director, 1967-69; *Chronicles Of Hell* (director); *Pantagleize* (co-director). The Acting Company — Co-Founder and Artistic Director, since 1972.
Broadway (Director: *Four Saints In Three Acts*, 1934; *Valley Forge*, 1934; *Lady From The Sea*, 1934; *Panic*, 1935; *Hamlet*, 1936; *Liberty Jones*, 1941; *Lute Song*, 1946; *King Lear*, 1950; *The Country Girl*, 1972; *Clarence Darrow*, 1974.
Also: Director, Drama Division of The Juilliard School, 1965-69; Producer of various films including *The Blue Dahlia, They Live By Night, The Bad And The Beautiful, Julius Caesar, Lust For Life, All Fall Down, Two Weeks In another Town;* appeared in the films *The Paper Chase, Rollerball* and *Three Days Of The Condor;* produced Playhouse 90 for television.
Awards: Academy (Oscar) Award for *The Paper Chase.*

BARNARD HUGHES, *Actor*
Born: July 16, 1915; Bedford Hills, New York
Theatre Companies: Equity Library Theatre — *A Bell For Adano, The Home Of The Brave* and *The Will And The Way*, 1957. American Place Theatre — *Hogan's Goat*, 1965. New York Shakespeare Festival — *Older People*, 1972; *Hamlet*, 1972; *Much Ado About Nothing* (also Broadway), 1972; *The Merry Wives Of Windsor*, 1974; *Pericles*, 1974. Circle In The Square — *Uncle Vanya*, 1973. Brooklyn Academy Of Music — *The Three Sisters*, 1977; *The Devil's Disciple*, 1978.
Broadway: *The Cat And The Canary*, 1937; *The Ivy Green*, 1949; *Dinosaur Wharf*, 1951; *A Majority Of One*, 1959; *Advise And Consent*, 1960; *The Advocate*, 1963; *Nobody*

Loves An Albatross, 1963; *Hamlet*, 1964; *I Was Dancing*, 1964; *Generation*, 1965; *How Now, Dow Jones*, 1967; *Wrong-Way Light Bulb*, 1969; *Sheep On The Runway*, 1970; *Abelard And Heloise*, 1971; *The Good Doctor*, 1973; *All Over Town*, 1974; *Da*, 1978.
Also: Appeared Off-Broadway in *Rosmersholm*, 1962 and *A Doll's House*, 1963; various films including *Midnight Cowboy, Where's Poppa* and *The Hospital;* numerous television appearances.
Awards: Tony Award — *Da*

MARYBETH HURT, *Actor*
Theatre Companies: New York Shakespeare Festival — *More Than You Deserve*, 1973; *As You Like It*, 1973; *Pericles*, 1974; *Trelawny Of The Wells*, 1975; *The Cherry Orchard*, 1977. Phoenix Theatre — *A Member Of The Wedding*, 1974; *Love For Love*, 1975; *Secret Service*, 1976; *Boy Meets Girl*, 1976. Ensemble Studio Theatre — *Studs Edsel*, 1974.
Awards: Clarence Derwent Award — *Love For Love.*

ANNE JACKSON, *Actor*
Born: September 3, 1926;
     Allegheny, Pennsylvania
Theatre Companies: American Repertory Theatre, 1946-47; *The Waltz Of The Toreadors* (Kennedy Center, Circle In The Square), 1973; *The Cherry Orchard* (Hartford Stage Company), 1975; *Absent Friends* (Long Wharf Theatre), 1977; *Marco Polo Sings A Solo* (New York Shakespeare Festival), 1977; Arena Stage (guest artist), 1977-78.
Broadway: *Summer And Smoke*, 1948; *Peter Pan*, 1950; *Lady From The Sea*, 1950; *Never Say Never*, 1951; *Oh Men! Oh Women!*, 1950 (tour, 1955); *Middle Of The Night*, 1956; *Major Barbara*, 1956; *Rhinoceros*, 1961; *Luv*, 1964; *The Exercise*, 1968; *The Front Page*, 1969; *Inquest*, 1970; *Promenade All*, 1972 (tour, 1971).
Off-Broadway: *Brecht On Brecht*, 1962; *The Typists And The Tiger*, 1963; *The Diary Of Anne Frank*, 1979.
Awards: Obie Award — *The Typists And The Tiger.*
Also: various film and television appearances.

BERNARD JACOBS, *Theatre Owner/ Producer*
Born: June 13, 1916; New York, N.Y.

The Shubert Organization: President, since 1972, of this theatrical organization which owns and operates seventeen theatres in New York, two in Chicago and one each in Boston, Philadelphia and Los Angeles; *The Shubert Organization* has also co-produced *Sherlock Holmes*, 1975; *Sly Fox*, 1976; *Fiddler On The Roof*, 1976; *The Act*, 1977; *The Gin Game*, 1977; *Ain't Misbehavin'*, 1978; *Richard III*, 1979.

Also: Vice President and Member Of The Board Of Governors, League Of New York Theatres and Producers, Inc.

JAMES EARL JONES, *Actor*
Born: January 13, 1931;
    Arkabutla, Mississippi

Theatre Companies: New York Shakespeare Festival — fifteen Shakespeare productions including the title roles in *Macbeth*, 1962 and 1966, *Othello*, 1964 and *King Lear*, 1973; *The Cherry Orchard*, 1972. Phoenix Theatre —*Next Time I'll Sing To You*, 1963; Repertory Theatre of Lincoln Center —*Danton's Death*, 1965. Negro Ensemble Company — *Happy Ending* and *Day Of Absence*, 1966. American Place Theatre—*The Displaced Person*, 1966. Arena Stage —*The Great White Hope*, 1967 (also Broadway, 1968); *The Bloodknot*, 1968. Goodman Memorial Theatre—*Othello*, 1968. Circle In The Square —*Boesman And Lena*, 1970; *The Iceman Cometh*, 1973. Mark Taper Forum—*Othello*, 1971.

Off-Broadway: various productions including *Wedding In Japan*, 1957; *The Blacks*, 1961; *Clandestine On The Morning Line*, 1961; *Moon On The Rainbow Shawl*, 1962; *The Bloodknot*, 1964; *Baal*, 1965.

Broadway: *Sunrise At Campobello*, 1958; *The Cool World*, 1960; *Infidel Caesar*, 1962; *A Hand Is On The Gate*, 1966; *Les Blancs*, 1970; *of Mice And Men*, 1974; *Paul Robeson*, 1978.

Also: *The Emperor Jones* (Boston Arts Festival, 1965 and European Tour, 1967): various films including *Dr. Strangelove, the Comedians, The Great White Hope* and *Claudine*; television appearances include *East Side/West Side, King Lear, The Cay, Jesus Of Nazareth* and *Roots, The Second Generation*.

Awards: Tony Award — *The Great White Hope*; Drama Desk Award—*Les Blancs*; Obie Awards—*Clandestine On The Morning Line, Othello, Baal*; Vernon Rice Award—*Othello*.

RAUL JULIA, *Actor*
Born: March 9, 1940; San Juan, Puerto Rico
Theatre Companies: New York Shakespeare Festival — *Macbeth*, 1966; *Titus Andronicus*, 1967; *The Memorandum*, 1968; *Two Gentlemen Of Verona* (also Broadway), 1971; *Hamlet*, 1972; *King Lear*, 1973; *As You Like It*, 1973; *The Emperor Of Late Night Radio*, 9173; *Threepenny Opera*, 1976; *The Cherry Orchard*, 1977; *The Taming Of The Shrew*, 1978; *Othello*, 1979. Phoenix Theatre — *The Persians*, 1970. American Place Theatre — *Pinkville*, 1971. Circle In The Square—*Where's Charley*, 1974.

Off-Broadway: *The Ox Cart*, 1966; *No Exit*, 1967; *Your Own Thing*, 1969; *The Castro Complex*, 1970; *Life Is A Dream*, 1972; *Blood Wedding*, 1973; *Frank Gagliano's City Scene, The Robber Bridegroom*, 1974.

Broadway: *The Cuban Thing*, 1968; *Indians*, 1969; *Via Galactica*, 1972; *Dracula*, 1979.

Also: various film and television appearances.

MADELINE KAHN, *Actor*
Born: September 29,
    Boston, Massachusetts

Broadway: *Two By Two*, 1970; *On The Twentieth Century*, 1978.

Theatre Companies: New York Shakespeare Festival — *Boom Boom Room*, 1973; *Marco Polo Sings A Solo*, 1977.

Also: *Promenade* (Off-Broadway), 1969; films include *What's Up Doc?, Paper Moon, Young Frankenstein, Blazing Saddles, High Anxiety*.

Awards — Drama Desk Award — *Boom Boom Room*.

MICHAEL KAHN, *Director*
Born: New York, New York

Off-Broadway: *The Love Nest*, 1963; *War*, 1964; *Funnyhouse Of A Negro*, 1964; *That 5 A.M. Jazz*, 1964; *The New Tenant* and *Victims Of Duty*, 1964; *Helen*, 1964; *The Owl Answers*, 1965; *America Hurrah!* (La Mama), 1965; *Thornton Wilder Plays*, 1966; *The Rimers Of Eldritch*, 1967; *Crimes Of Passion*, 1969; *Women Beware Women*, 1972; *Friend*, 1973.

Theatre Companies: New York Shakespeare Festival—*Measure For Measure*, 1966. Cincinnati Playhouse In The Park — *The Cavern*, 1967 and *Camino Real*, 1968. American Shakespeare Theatre — Artistic Director, 1969-74 and director of numerous productions including *Henry V* (also Broadway), 1969; *Othello* (also Broadway), 1970; *Mourning Becomes Electra*, 1971; *Macbeth*, 1973; *Measure For Measure*, 1973; *Cat On A Hot Tin Roof* (also Broadway), 1974; *The Winter's Tale*, 1975; *Our Town*, 1975; *As You Like It*, 1976. Goodman Theatre—*Old Times*, 1972 and *Tooth Of Crime*, 1974. McCarter Theatre—Producing Director since 1974 and director of various productions including *Beyond The Horizon*, 1974; *Mother Courage*, 1975; *A Streetcar Named Desire*, 1976; *The Heiress*, 1976; *A Grave Under taking*, 1975; *Section Nine*, 1975; *The Night Of The Tribades* (also Broadway), 1977. The Acting Company—artistic Director since 1977; also founding member of the Drama Division of the Juilliard School.

Broadway: *The Death Of Bessie Smith*, 1968; *Here's Where I Belong*, 1968.

Awards: Saturday Review Award—*Measure For Measure*.

JOHN KANDER, *Composer*
Born: March 18, 1927; Kansas City, Missouri
With Fred Ebb as Lyricist: *Flora, The Red Menace*, 1965; *Cabaret*, 1966; *The Happy Time*, 1968; *Zorba*, 1968; *70 Girls 70*, 1971; *Chicago*, 1975; *2 x 5*, 1976; *The Act*, 1977.
Also: *A Family Affair*, 1962; *Never Too Late* (incidental music), 1962.
Awards: Tony Award—*Cabaret*

CAROL KANE, *Actor*
Born: 1952; Cleveland, Ohio
Theatre Companies: New York Shakespeare Festival — *The Tempest*, 1974; *Macbeth*, 1974; *The Resistible Rise Of Arturo Ui*, 1974; *Gogol*, 1976. The Company—*Waiting For Godot*, 1977.
Also: appeared in Broadway in *Ring Round The Bathtub*, 1972 and *The Effect Of Gamma Rays on Man-in-the-Moon Marigolds*, 1978; *The Enchanted* (Kennedy Center), 1973; films include *Carnal Knowledge, The Last Detail, Hester Street, Dog Day Afternoon*.

STACY KEACH, *Actor*
Born: June 2, 1941; Savannah, Georgia
Theatre Companies: Oregon Shakespeare Festival — 1962 and 1963 seasons. New York Shakespeare Festival—*Hamlet*, 1964; *Henry IV, Parts 1 and 2*, 1968; *Peer Gynt*, 1969;

Hamlet, 1972. Repertory Theatre Of Lincoln Center—*Danton's Death*, 1965; *The Country Wife*, 1965; *Caucasian Chalk Circle*, 1966; *King Lear*, 1968. Long Wharf Theatre — *The Three Sisters*, 1966; *Oh, What A Lovely War*, 1966; *Hamlet*, 1972. Yale Repertory Theatre —*We Bombed In New Haven*, 1967; *Henry IV, The Three Sisters* and *Coriolanus*, 1968. Arena Stage—*Indians* (also Broadway), 1969. Mark Taper Forum—*Hamlet, 1974*.
Off-Broadway: *MacBird!*, 1967; *The Niggerlovers*, 1967; *Long Day's Journey Into Night*, 1971.
Broadway: *Deathtrap*, 1978.
Also: films include *The Heart Is A Lonely Hunter, The End Of The Road, Brewster McCloud, Luther, Conduct Unbecoming*; various television appearances.
Awards: Obie and Vernon Rice Awards — *MacBird!, Long Day's Journey Into Night, Hamlet*.

WALTER KERR, *Theatre Critic*
Born: July 8, 1913; Evanston, Illinois
Drama Critic: *Commonwealth Magazine*, 1950-52; *New York Herald Tribune*, 1951-66; *New York Times*, since 1966.
Author/Director: *Sing Out Sweet Land*, 1944; *Touch And Go* (Co-Author), 1949; *Goldilocks* (Co-Author), 1959.
Published Works: *How Not To Write A Play, Criticism and Censorship, Pieces At Eight, The Decline Of Pleasure, Theatre In Spite Of Itself, Journey Into The Centre Of The Theatre*.
Awards: George Jean Nathan Drama Criticism Award, American Academy Of Arts And Letters Literature Award, National Institute Of Arts And Letters Literature Award.

WOODIE KING, JR., *Producer/Director*
Born: July 27, 1937; Alabama
New Federal Theatre (Henry Street Settlement): Director since 1973 and Artistic Director, Henry Street Settlement, 1970-73, where he produced several of the plays listed below.
Producer: *A Black Quartet*, 1969; *Slaveship* (Co-Producer with Chelsea Theatre Center), 1969; *Behold Cometh The VanDerk Kellans*, 1970; *In New England Winters*, 1971; *Black Girl*, 1971; *What The Winesellers Buy*, 1973 (Co-Producer with the New York Shakespeare Festival, 1974); *The Prodigal Sister*, 1974; *The Fabulous Miss Marie* (Philadelphia), 1975;

The Taking Of Miss Janie, 1974 (Co-Producer with the New York Shakespeare Festival, 1975); *Medal Of Honor Rag* (Co-Producer), 1976; *Showdown Time*, 1976; *For Colored Girls Who Have Considered Suicide/When The Rainbow Is Enuf* (Co-Producer with the New York Shakespeare Festival), 1976.

Director: various productions at Concert East Theatre (which he co-founded), 1969-63 including *Study In Color, The Slave* and *The Toilet, God's Trombone, Zoo Story, The Connection, The Death Of Bessie Smith; Study In Color* (Theatre Genesis), 1964; *The Weary Blues* (Lincoln Center), 1965; *The Warning* (Gate Theatre), 1969; *What The Winesellers Buy* (New Federal Theatre), 1973; *Sizwe Banzi Is Dead* (Pittsburgh Public Theatre, 1976 and Buffalo Studio Arena, 1977); *The First Breeze Of Summer* (Baltimore Center Stage), 1977; *Daddy* (New Federal Theatre), 1977; *Cockfight* (American Place Theatre), 1977; *A Raisin In The Sun* (Geva, Rochester), 1978.

Also: produced the films *The Black Theatre Movement* (also director), *Right On, Epitaph, The Long Night* (Co-Producer, also Director); Cultural Arts Director, Mobilization For Youth, 1965-70; Drama Critic, Detroit Tribune, 1959-62.

Awards: Obie Award — *Special Citation to Henry Street Settlement*, 1975; New York Drama Critics Award — *The Taking Of Miss Janie*; Audelco Award — *Producer Of The Year*, 1977.

SHIRLEY KNIGHT, *Actor*
Born: July 5, 1936; Goessel, Kansas

Broadway: *The Three Sisters*, 1964; *We Have Always Lived In The Castle*, 1966; *The Watering Place*, 1969; *Kennedy's Children*, 1975.

Off-Broadway: *Journey To The Day*, 1963; *Rooms*, 1966.

Theatre Companies: *And People All Around* (Bristol Old Vic), 1967; *A Streetcar Named Desire* (McCarter Theatre), 1976; *Happy End* (Chelsea Theatre Center), 1977; *Landscape Of The Body* (New York Shakespeare Festival), 1977.

England: *A Touch Of The Poet* (Gardner Arts Centre), 1970; *Antigone* (London), 1971; *Economic Necessity* (New Haymarket Theatre, Leicester).

Also: *Look Back In Anger* (Pasadena Playhouse), 1958; *Dutchman* (Warner Playhouse, Los Angeles), 1965; various films including *The Dark At The Top Of The Stairs, Sweet Bird Of Youth, The Group, Dutchman* and *Petulia;* numerous television appearances.

Awards: Tony Award—*Kennedy's Children*

LAWRENCE KORNFELD, *Director*
Born: 1930; New York, New York

Theatre Companies: The Living Theatre — General Manager and Assistant Director, 1957-61; directed *Purgatory, A Full Moon In March, Theory Of Comedy.* Judson Poets Theatre—Co-Founder and Resident Director, 1961-78; directed over thirty productions including *Home Movies* (also Off-Broadway, 1964), *Corilla Queen* (also Off-Broadway, 1967), *In Circles* (also Off-Broadway, 1967), *Peace* (also Off-Broadway, 1969), *Promenade* (also Off-Broadway, 1969) and *Wanted* (also Off-Broadway, 1972). Theatre For The New City, Co-Founder and Artistic Director, 1970-72; directed *Keeper Of The Hippo Horn, Dracula/Sabbat.* American Place Theatre — *Jonah*, 1966. Arena Stage — *A Look At The Fifties*, 1972-73 season. Yale Repertory Theatre — *General Gorgeous*, 1975-76 season. Guthrie Theatre — *And Things That Go Bump In The Night.* New York Theatre Strategy—*He Want Shih, Lines Of Vision.*

Also: *Minnie's Boys* (Broadway), 1970; *The Duel* (Metropolitan Opera Young People's Program).

Awards: Obie Awards—*Distinguished Direction* 1964, 1971, 1975.

SWOOZIE KURTZ, *Actor*
Born: September 6, 1944; Omaha, Nebraska

Off-Broadway: *Firebugs*, 1968; *The Effects Of Gamma Rays On Man-In-The-Moon Marigolds*, 1970; *Enter A Free Man*, 1974.

Threatre Companies: Long Wharf Theatre — 1973-74 season; *On The Outside*, 1975. Manhattan Theatre Club — *Hopscotch* and *Spared*, 1974; *Life Class*, 1975; *Children*, 1976. Goodman Theatre — *The Philanthropist*, 1974. Circle In The Square — *Ah, Wilderness*, 1975; *Tartuffe*, 1977. Arena Stage —1976-77 season including *A History Of The American Film* (also Broadway, 1978); New York Shakespeare Festival—*Museum*, 1977. Phoenix Theatre —*Uncommon Women And Others*, 1977. Hartman Theatre Company—*The Middle Ages*, 1978.

ANGELA LANSBURY, *Actor*
Born: October 16, 1925; London, England
Broadway: *Hotel Paradiso,* 1957; *A Taste Of Honey,* 1960; *Anyone Can Whistle,* 1964; *Mame,* 1966; *Dear World,* 1969; *Gypsy,* 1974; *Sweeny Todd,* 1979.
Also: Over thirty-five films including *Gaslight, National Velvet, The Picture Of Dorian Gray, The Long Hot Summer, The Dark At The Top Of The Stairs, The Manchurian Candidate, The World Of Henry Orient, Death On The Nile.*
Awards: Tony Awards — *Gypsy, Sweeny Todd.*

ALAN JAY LERNER, *Playwright/Lyricist*
Born: August 31, 1918; New York, New York
Book And Lyrics: *The Day Before Spring,* 1945; *Brigadoon,* 1947; *Paint Your Wagon,* 1951; *My Fair Lady,* 1956; *Camelot* (also co-producer), 1960; *On A Clear Day You Can See Forever* (also co-producer), 1965; *Coco,* 1969; *Gigi,* 1973; *1600 Pennsylvania Avenue,* 1976; *Carmelita,* 1979.
Also: in addition to film versions of several of these stage musicals, screenplays of *An American In Paris,* screenplay and lyrics for *Royal Wedding* and *The Little Prince.*
Awards: Tony Awards — *My Fair Lady, Gigi* (score); New York Drama Critics Awards — *Brigadoon, My Fair Lady;* Donaldson Award — *May Fair Lady;* Academy (Oscar) Awards— *An American In Paris, Gigi.*

ROBERT LEWIS, *Director/Actor/Producer*
Born: March 16, 1909; New York, New York
Actor: Civic Repertory Theatre, 1929-31; Group Theatre Company 1931-37.
Director: *Golden Boy* (tour), 1938; *My Heart's In The Highlands,* 1939; *Heavenly Express,* 1940; *Five Alarm Waltz,* 1941; *Mexican Mural* (also producer), 1942; *Land's End,* 1946; *Brigadoon,* 1947; *Regina,* 1949; *The Happy Time,* 1950; *The Grass Harp,* 1952; *The Teahouse Of The August Moon,* 1953; *Witness For The Prosecution,* 1954; *Mister Johnson* (also co-producer), 1956; *The Hidden River,* 1957; *Jamaica,* 1957; *A Handful Of Fire,* 1958; *Cheri* (also co-producer), 1959; *Kwamina,* 1961; *Foxy,* 1964; *On A Clear Day You Can See Forever,* 1965; *Traveler Without Luggage,* 1964.
Theatre Companies: directed *Crimes* and *Crimes* (Yale Repertory Theatre), 1970; *The*
Connection, The Sea Gull (Center Stage), 1971.
Also: Director, Group Theatre Studio; Co-founder, Actors' Studio; Director, Robert Lewis Theatre Workshop; author of *Method Or Madness.*
Awards: NY Drama Critics Award — *The Teahouse Of The August Moon.*

JOHN LITHGOW, *Actor/Director*
Born: October 19, 1945; Rochester, New York
Theatre Companies: Antioch Shakespeare Festival — *A Midsummer Night's Dream,* 1953. Great Lakes Shakespeare Festival — fifteen Shakespearean roles, 1963-64 season. McCarter Theatre — *Pygmalion, Of Mice And Men, Troilus And Cressida,* 1969-70 season. Bucks County Playhouse — *Hadrian VII, The Roar Of The Greasepaint, The Magistrate,* 1970 season; Long Wharf Theatre — *Trelawny Of The Wells, The Changing Room* (also Broadway, 1973) and *What Price Glory,* 1972; *Spokesong* (also Circle In The Square), 1979. New York Shakespeare Festival — *Hamlet,* 1975; *Trelawny Of The Wells,* 1975. Phoenix Theatre — *A Memory Of Two Mondays,* 1976; *Secret Service,* 1976.
Broadway: *My Fat Friend,* 1974; *Comedians,* 1976; *Anna Christie,* 1977.
Director: McCarter Theatre — *As You Like It,* 1968; *Much Ado About Nothing,* 1969; *The Way Of The World,* 1970. Bucks County Playhouse — *The Magistrate, Barefoot In The Park,* 1970. Baltimore Center Stage — *The Beaux' Strategem,* 1972. Long Wharf Theatre — *A Pagan Place,* 1973. Phoenix Theatre — *Boy Meets Girl,* 1976.
Awards: Tony and Drama Desk Awards — *The Changing Room.*

CLEAVON LITTLE, *Actor*
Born: June 1, 1939; Chickasha, Oklahoma
Theatre Companies: *Macbeth,* 1966 and *Hamlet,* 1968 (New York Shakespeare Festival); *Narrow Road To The Deep North* (Repertory Theatre Of Lincoln Center), 1972; *The Charlatan* (Mark Taper Forum), 1973; *The Great Macdaddy* (Negro Ensemble Company), 1974.
Broadway: *Jimmy Shine,* 1968; *Purlie,* 1970; *All Over Town,* 1974; *The Poison Tree,* 1976.
Off-Broadway: *Americana,* 1966; *MacBird,* 1967; *Scuba Duba,* 1967; *Someone's Comin' Hungry,* 1969; *The Ofay Watcher,* 1969.

Also: Several films including *Cotton Comes To Harlem* and *Blazing Saddles* and television appearances.
Awards: Tony Award—*Purlie.*

SANTO LOQUASTO, *Designer*
Born: July 26, 1944;
      Wilkes-Barre, Pennsylvania
Theatre Companies: Harford Stage Company — settings for various productions, 1968-70, 1974-77; Yale Repertory Theatre—four productions, 1970. New York Shakespeare Festival — since 1971 over twenty set designs including on Broadway: *Sticks and Bones,* 1971; *That Championship Season,* 1972; *Miss Margarida's Way,* 1977 and at Lincoln Center: *Boom Boom Room,* 1973; *Mert And Phil,* 1974; *What The Winesellers Buy,* 1974; *The Dance Of Death,* 1974; *Hamlet,* 1975; *The Cherry Orchard* (also costumes), 1978. Long Wharf Theatre—*Tiny Alice,* 1968; *Skin Of Our Teeth,* 1970. Mark Taper Forum—*Old Times,* 1972. Arena Stage —*The House Of Blue Leaves,* 1972; *Uptight,* 1972; various productions 1975-78.
Broadway: *The Secret Affairs Of Mildred Wild,* 1972; *Kennedy's Children,* 1975; *Murder Among Friends,* 1975; *Legend,* 1976; *Golda,* 1977; *American Buffalo,* 1977; *The Mighty Gents,* 1978; *King Of Hearts,* 1978.
Also: *The Unseen Hand* and *Forensic And The Navigators* (Off-Broadway), 1970; designs for *Twyla Tharp Dance Company, The Joffrey Ballet, New York City Ballet.*
Awards: Tony Award—*The Cherry Orchard* (costumes); Drama Desk Awards — *That Championship Season, Sticks And Bones;* Maharam Award—*Agamemnon.*

CHARLES LUDLAM, *Playwright/Actor/ Director*
Ridiculous Theatrical Company: founder, 1967. Author/Director/Actor—*When Queens Collide,* 1967; *Big Hotel,* 1967; *Bluebeard (La Mama),* 1970; *Corn,* 1972; *Eunuchs Of The Forbidden City* (Theatre For The New City), 1972; *Camille* (adaptation), 1973; *Hot Ice,* 1974; *Stage Blood,* 1974; *Tatu Tableaux,* 1975. Author/Director—*Whores Of Babylon* (Co-Author), 1968; *Caprice* (Performing Garage), 1976; *Der Ring Gott Forblonjet,* 1977. *The Enchanted Pig,* 1979. Director/Actor — *The Grand Tarot,* 1971. Co-Author—*Turds In Hell,* 1968.

DAVID MAMET, *Playwright*
Born: November 30, 1947; Chicago, Illinois
Chicago: *Duck Variations* (The Body Politic), 1972; *Sexual Perversity In Chicago* (Organic Theatre), 1974; *Squirrels* (St. Nicholas Theatre), 1974; *American Buffalo* (Goodman Theatre), 1975; *A Life In The Theatre* (Goodman Theatre), 1977; *The Water Engine* (St. Nicholas Theatre), 1977; *The Woods* (St. Nicholas Theatre), 1977.
New York: *Duck Variations* and *Sexual Perversity In Chicago* (St. Clements Theatre, 1976; Off-Broadway, 1977); *American Buffalo* (Boradway), 1977; *A Life In The Theatre* (Off-Broadway), 1977; *The Water Engine* (New York Shakespeare Festival, also Broadway), 1978; *The Woods* (New York Shakespeare Festival), 1979.
Children's Plays: *Mackinac* (Center Youth Theatre), 1972; *The Poet And The Rent* (St. Nicholas Theatre, 1974; Circle Rep., 1979); *The Revenge Of The Space Pandas* (St. Nicholas Theatre), 1977.
Also: *Reunion* and *Dark Pony* (Yale Repertory Theatre), 1977; founding member and former Artistic Director, St. Nicholas Theatre.

Awards: Joseph Jefferson Award — *Sexual Perversity In Chicago;* Obie Award — *Best New Playwright,* 1975; New York Drama Critics Award—*American Buffalo.*

MARSHALL MASON, *Director*
Born: February 24, 1940; Amarillo, Texas
Theatre Companies: *Cafe Cino* (1962-64) — *The Rue Garden, The Clown, Romance D'Amour, The Haunted Host.* Cafe La Mama (1965-67) *Balm In Gilead, The Sand Castle, A Coffee Ground Among Tea Leaves.* American Theatre Project (1968) — founder and director. Circle Theatre Company (since 1969) founder and artistic director, directed *The Three Sisters,* 1970; *Sextet (Yes),* 1971; *Elephant In The House,* 1972; *The Hot L Baltimore,* 1973; *Prodigal,* 1973; *The Sea Horse,* 1974; *Battle Of Angels,* 1974; *Harry Outside,* 1975; *The Mound Builders,* 1975; *The Elephant In The House,* 1975; *Knock, Knock* (also Broadway), 1976; *Serenading Louie,* 1976; *A Tribute To Lili Lamont,* 1976; *A Farm,* 1976; *Mrs. Murray's Farm,* 1976; *My Life,* 1977; *Ulysses In Nighttown,* 1977; *The Fifth Of July,* 1978; *Talley's Folly,* 1979.
Off-Broadway: *One Room With Bath,* 1967;

Untitled Play, 1968; *Goodnight, I Love You*, 1968; *Little Eyolf*, 1964; *Arms And The Man*, 1968; *Home Free*, 1965; *Spring Play*, 1968; *The Gingham Dog*, 1968.
Also: Producer of *When You Comin' Back, Red Ryder*, 1973; directed *Come Back, Little Sheba* (Queens Playhouse), 1974.
Awards: Obie Award—*The Hot L Baltimore*.

LYNNE MEADOW, *Producer/Director*
Born: November 12, 1946;
    New Haven, Connecticut
Manhattan Theatre Club: Artistic Director since 1972; produced well over one hundred works including *Boccaccio, Canadian Gothic/American Modern, Charlie The Chicken* and *Master Class, Little Mahagonny, Bad Habits* (1972-73 season); *Waiting For Lefty*, 1973; *A Circle Of Sound*, 1973; *Little Eyolf*, 1974; *The Breasts Of Tiresias*, 1974; *Candle In The Wind*, 1974; *The Morning After Optimism*, 1974; *The Wager*, 1974; *The Sirens*, 1974; *Naomi Court*, 1974; *End Of Summer*, 1974; *Bits And Pieces*, 1974; *The Seagull*, 1975; *The Runner Stumbles*, 1975; *The Sea*, 1975; *Life Class*, 1975; *The Blood Knot*, 1976; *Ashes* (co-production with the New York Shakespeare Festival), 1976; *The Last Street Play*, 1977; *Catsplay*, 1978; *Ain't Misbehavin'* (also Broadway), 1978; also various operas, musical and cabaret events and poetry series.
Director: for the Manhattan Theatre Club various productions including *Jesus As Seen By His Friends*, 1973; *Shooting Gallery*, 1973; *The Wager*, 1974; *Bits And Pieces*, 1974; *Golden Boy*, 1975; *Ashes*, 1976; *Chez Nous*, 1977; *Artichoke*, 1978; *Catsplay*, 1978; also *Marco Polo* (Phoenix Theatre).
Awards: Outer Critics' Circle Award—*1977 to Lynne Meadow*; Obie Award—*Ashes*.

MICHAEL MORIARTY, *Actor*
Born: April 5, 1941; Detroit, Michigan
Theatre Companies: New York Shakespeare Festival — *The Winter's Tale*, 1963; *Antony And Cleopatra*, 1963; *Love's Labour's Lost*, 1965; *Troilus And Cressida*, 1965; *Richard III*, 1974; *Henry V*, 1976. Guthrie Theatre — various productions, 1966-70 including *Enrico IV, The House Of Atreus* (also Broadway), *The Resistible Rise Of Arturo Ui* (also Broadway), *Mourning Becomes Electra*. Charles Playhouse — *Major Barbara*, 1966; *In The Jungle Of Cities*, 1970.

Alley Theatre—*The Night Thoreau Spent In Jail*, 1971. Brooklyn Academy Of Music — *Long Day's Journey Into Night*, 1976. New Dramatists — *The Wakefield Plays*, 1976; Actors' Studio—*Alfred Dies*, 1977 and *Alfred The Great* 1978.
Broadway: *Trial Of The Catonsville Nine*, 1971; *Find Your Way Home*, 1974; *G.R. Point*, 1979.
Also: *Peanut Butter And Jelly* (Off-Broadway), 1971; television appearances include *The Glass Menagerie* and *Holocaust*; films include *Bang The Drum Slowly* and *The Last Detail*.
Awards: Tony and Drama Desk Awards — *Find Your Way Home*.

ZERO MOSTEL, *Actor*
Born: February 28, 1915; Brooklyn, New York (Died: Sept. 8, 1977)
Broadway: *Keep 'Em Laughing*, 1942; *Concert Varieties*, 1945; *Beggars Holiday*, 1946; *Flight Into Egypt*, 1952; *Good As Gold*, 1957; *Rhinocerus*, 1961; *A Funny Thing Happened On The Way To The Forum*, 1962; *Fiddler On The Roof*, 1962; *Ulysses In Nighttown*, 1974; *Fiddler On The Roof*, 1976.
Off-Broadway: *A Stone For Danny Fisher*, 1954; *The Good Woman Of Setzuan* (Phoenix), 1956; *Ulysses In Nighttown*, 1958.
Also: various films including *Dubarry Was A Lady, Panic In The Streets, A Funny Thing Happened On The Way To The Forum, The Producers, The Angel Levine, Hot Rock, The Front*.
Awards: Tony Awards — *Rhinoceros, A Funny Thing Happened On The Way To The Forum*; New York Drama Critics Award — *Fiddler On The Roof*; Obie Award—*Ulysses In Nighttown*.

THARON MUSSER, *Lighting Designer*
Born: January 8, 1925; Roanoke, Virginia
Broadway: numerous designs include *Long Day's Journey Into Night*, 1956; *J.B.*, 1958; *The Entertainer*, 1958; *Mother Courage*, 1963; *Here's Love*, 1963; *Any Wednesday*, 1964; *Golden Boy*, 1964; *Kelly*, 1965; *Flora, The Red Menace*, 1965; *A Delicate Balance*, 1966; *The Lion In Winter*, 1966; *Mame*, 1966; *Hallelujah, Baby*, 1967; *The Birthday Party*, 1967; *Applause*, 1970; *The Prisoner Of Second Avenue*, 1971; *Follies*, 1971; *The Trial Of The Catonsville Nine*, 1971; *The Sunshine*

Boys, 1972; *The Creation Of The World And Other Business*, 1972; *A Little Night Music*, 1973; *The Good Doctor*, 1973; *God's Favorite*, 1974; *Scapino*, 1974; *Mack And Mabel*, 1974; *Candide*, 1974; *The Wiz*, 1975; *Same Time, Next Year*, 1975; *Me And Bessie*, 1975; *A Chorus Line*, 1975; *Pacific Overtures*, 1976; *1600 Pennsylvania Avenue*, 1976; *California Suite*, 1976; *Chapter Two*, 1977; *Ballroom*, 1978.

Theatre Companies: American Shakespeare Theatre, 1958-68; National Repertory Theatre, 1961-67; Dallas Civic Opera, various productions since 1969; Mark Taper Forum, various productions since 1970.

Awards: Tony Awards — *Follies, A Chorus Line.*

TOM O'HORGAN, *Director*
Born: May 3, 1926; Chicago, Illinois

Off-Off-Broadway: Cafe Cino — *Lover And Vexation* (also author), 1963. Cafe La Mama — *The Maids*, 1964; *The Hessian Corporal*, 1966; *Futz* (also composer), 1967; *Tom Paine* (also composer), 1967; name Artistic Director of La Mama, ETC, 1969.

Broadway: *Hair*, 1968; *Lenny*, 1971; *Jesus Christ Superstar*, 1971; *Inner City* (also conceived and produced), 1971; *Dude*, 1972; *Sgt. Pepper's Lonely Hearts Club Band*, 1974; *The Leaf People* (New York Shakespeare Festival), 1975.

Also: Composer for *The Tempest*, 1959 and four *Second City* revues, 1963-64.

Awards: Drama Desk Awards — *Tom Paine, Lenny;* Obie Award — *Futz.*

JOSEPH PAPP, *Producer/Director*
(Founder, Producer — New York Shakespeare Festival)
Born: June 22, 1921; Brooklyn, New York

Early Years: Emmanuel Presbyterian Church (Shakespeare Workshop), 1955-56; East River Amphitheatre (first summer of Free Shakespeare), 1956; Heckscher Theatre, 1957-59.

Free Shakespeare in Central Park: originated on first Mobile Stage, 1957; at Belvedere Lake, 1958-60; Wollman Rink, 1961; Delacorte Theatre since 1962. Over fifty productions representing all of Shakespeare's plays (except *Henry VIII*) as well as five non-Shakespearean works (Sophocles' *Electra, Peer Gynt, Ti-Jean And His Brothers, Threepenny Opera, Agamemnon*).

Mobile Theatre: Touring parks and playgrounds of New York City since 1964; over twenty-five productions including seven Shakespeare plays, seven contemporary works, as well as children's shows and Spanish language productions.

Public Theatre: in over 150 productions since 1967, starting with the original production of *Hair*, over 100 new plays produced by American writers including *Thomas Babe, Ed Bullins, Alice Childress, Charles Gordone, John Guare, Tina Howe, Adrienne Kennedy, Myrna Lamb, David Mamet, Jason Miller, Susan Miller, Robert Montgomery, John Ford Noonan, Miguel Pinero, David Rabe, Dennis Reardon, Ntozake Shange, Wallace Shawn, Sam Shepard, Elizabeth Swados, Michael Weller, Richard Wesley, Edgar White.*

Broadway: *Two Gentlemen Of Verona*, 1971 and *Much Ado About Nothing*, 1972 transferred from Central Park; *Sticks And Bones*, 1971; *That Championship Season*, 1972; *A Chorus Line*, 1975; *For Colored Girls Who Have Considered Suicide /When The Rainbow Is Enuf*, 1977; *Miss Margarida's Way*, 1977; *The Water Engine*, 1978; *Runaways*, 1978 transferred from Public Theatre.

Lincoln Center: Theatre constituent, 1973-78. New plays produced at the Beaumont Theatre include *Boom Boom Room*, 1973; *The Au Pair Man*, 1973; *What The Winesellers Buy*, 1974; *Short Eyes*, 1974; *Mert And Phil*, 1974; *Black Picture Show*, 1975; and *The Taking Of Miss Janie*, 1975 and *Streamers*, 1976 at the Newhouse. Classics include *The Dance Of Death*, 1974; *A Doll's House*, 1975; *Trelawny Of The Wells*, 1975; *Hamlet*, 1975; *Mrs. Warren's Profession*, 1976; *Threepenny Opera*, 1976; *The Cherry Orchard*, 1977; *Agamemnon*, 1977; and five Shakespeare plays at the Newhouse.

Director: *Cymbeline*, 1955; *The Changeling*, 1956; *Twelfth Night*, 1958; *Henry V*, 1960; *Much Ado About Nothing*, 1961; *Julius Caesar*, 1962; *The Merchant Of Venice*, 1962; *King Lear*, 1962; *Antony And Cleopatra*, 1963; *Twelfth Night*, 1963; *Hamlet*, 1964; *Henry V*, 1965; *All's Well That Ends Well*, 1966; *King John*, 1967; *The Memorandum*, 1968; *Hamlet*, 1968; *Romeo And Juliet*, 1968; *Huui, Huui*, 1968; *Twelfth Night*, 1969; *Mod Donna*, 1969; *As You Like It*, 1973; *Mert And Phil*, 1974; *Apple Pie*, 1975; *Henry V*, 1976.

Also: *The Merchant Of Venice, Antony And*

Cleopatra, Hamlet, Much Ado About Nothing, Sticks And Bones, Wedding Band (also director) and *King Lear* produced for television.

Awards. Pulitzer Prizes — *No Place To Be Somebody, That Championship Season, A Chorus Line;* Tony Awards — *Two Gentlemen Of Verona, Sticks And Bones, That Championship Season, A Chorus Line.* New York Drama Critics Awards — *Two Gentlemen Of Verona, That Championship Season, Sticks And Bones* (citation), *Short Eyes, The Taking Of Miss Janie, A Chorus Line;* Obie Awards — *Short Eyes, The Memorandum, The Basic Training Of Pavlo Hummel, The Taking Of Miss Janie, Ashes,* Special Citation (1956). Awards to Joseph Papp — Margo Jones Award, 1971; Handel Medallion, 1971; New York State Award, 1972; Special Obie, 1975.

ESTELLE PARSONS, *Actor*
Born: November 20, 1927;
    Lynn, Massachusetts

Broadway: *Happy Hunting,* 1956; *Beg, Borrow Or Steal,* 1960; *Ready When You Are, C.B.,* 1964; *Malcolm,* 1966; *The Seven Descents Of Myrtle,* 1968; *And Miss Reardon Drinks A Little,* 1971; *The Norman Conquests,* 1975; *Ladies At The Alamo,* 1977.

Off-Broadway: *The Threepenny Opera,* 1960; *Automobile Graveyard,* 1961; *Mrs. Dally Has A Lover,* 1962; *In The Summer House,* 1964; *Monopoly,* 1970; *Mahagony,* 1970.

Theatre Companies: Phoenix Theatre — *Next Time I'll Sing To You,* 1963; Cincinnati Playhouse In The Park—1965 season; *Honor And Offer,* 1968. Berkshire Playhouse—1966 (inaugural) season. Repertory Theatre Of Lincoln Center—*East Wind,* 1967; *Galileo,* 1967; *People Are Living There,* 1974. Yale Repertory Theatre — *We Bombed In New Haven,* 1967; *Man Is Man,* 1978. Philadelphia Playhouse In The Park—*A Taste Of Honey,* 1968. New York Shakespeare Festival—*Peer Gynt,* 1969; *Barbary Shore,* 1973; *Mert And Phil,* 1974; *Miss Margarida's Way* (also Broadway), 1977. Actor's Studio — *Silent Partner,* 1972; *Oh Glorious Tintinnabulation,* 1974. Hartman Theatre Company — *The Reason We Eat,* 1977. Buffalo Studio Arena—*Who's Afraid Of Virginia Woolf,* 1978.

Also: films include *Bonnie And Clyde, Rachel, Rachel, Watermelon Man, I Never Sang For My Father, For Pete's Sake;* writer

and commentator for the *Today Show* (1953-55) and various other television appearances.

Awards: Obie Awards — *In The Summer House, Next Time I'll Sing To You;* Academy (Oscar) Award—*Bonnie And Clyde.*

ROBERT PATRICK, *Playwright*
Born: September 27, 1937; Kilgore, Texas

Off-Off-Broadway: author of over forty plays produced at: Cafe Cino—seven plays including *Haunted House,* 1964 and *Lights Camera Action,* 1966. La Mama — six plays including *Mirage,* 1965 and *Play By Play,* 1972. Old Reliable Theatre — eighteen plays including *Salvation Army,* 1968; *Fog,* 1969; *Joyce Dynel,* 1969. The Dove Company — three plays, 1970; Workshop Of The Players Art — three plays including *Mercy Drop,* 1973. Spring Street Company—*The Golden Circle,* 1972; New York Theatre Ensemble — *Something Else,* 1973.

Also: directed, performed in or wrote songs for most of the above.

Broadway: *Kennedy's Children,* 1975.

ROBERT PRESTON, *Actor*
Born: June 8, 1918;
    Newton Highlands, Massachusetts

Broadway: *Twentieth Century,* 1951; *Men Of Distinction,* 1953; *His And Hers,* 1954; *The Tender Trap,* 1954; *Janus,* 1955; *The Hidden River,* 1957; *The Music Man,* 1957; *Nobody Loves An Albatross,* 1963; *Ben Franklin In Paris,* 1964; *The Lion In Winter,* 1966; *I Do! I Do!,* 1966; *Mack And Mabel,* 1974; *Sly Fox,* 1977.

Also: *Kearney From Killarney,* 1932 and *Julius Caesar,* 1936 in Los Angeles; various roles at the Pasadena Playhouse, 1937-38; *The Play's The Thing* (18 Actors Company), 1949; *The Male Animal* (New York City Center), 1952; *Too True To Be Good* (Off-Broadway), 1963; numerous films including *Beau Geste, This Gun For Hire, Blood On The Moon; The Sundowners, The Dark At The Top Of The Stairs, The Music Man, All The Way Home, Mame;* numerous television appearances.

Awards: Tony Awards — *The Music Man, I Do! I Do!*

HAL PRINCE, *Producer/Director*
Born: January 30, 1928; New York, New York

Producer/Director: *She Loves Me* (Co-Producer), 1963; *It's A Bird...It's A Plane... It's Superman,* 1966; *Cabaret,* 1966; *Zorba,* 1968; *Company,* 1970; *Follies* (Co-Director), 1971; *A Little Night Music,* 1973; *Pacific Overtures,* 1976.

Producer: *The Pajama Game* (Co-Producer), 1954; *Damn Yankees* (Co-Producer), 1955; *New Girl In Town* (Co-Producer), 1957; *West Side Story* (Co-Producer), 1957; *Fiorello,* 1959; *Tenderloin,* 1960; *A Call On Kuprin,* 1961; *Take Her She's Mine,* 1961; *A Funny Thing Happened On The Way To The Forum,* 1962; *Fiddler On The Roof,* 1964; *Flora, The Red Menace,* 1965; *Side By Side By Sondheim,* 1977.

Director: *A Family Affair,* 1962; *Baker Street,* 1965; *Some Of My Best Friends,* 1977; *On The Twentieth Century,* 1978; *Sweeny Todd,* 1979.

Theatre Companies (director): Phoenix Theatre—*The Matchmaker,* 1963; *The Great God Brown,* 1972; *The Visit,* 1973; *Holiday,* 1973; *Love For Love,* 1974. Chelsea Theatre Center — *Candide,* 1973 (co-produced on Broadway, 1974).

Awards: Tony Awards — Producer/Director: *Cabaret, Company, Candide;* Producer: *The Pajama Game, Damn Yankees, Fiorello, A Funny Thing Happened On The Way To The Forum, Fiddler On The Roof, Cabaret, Company, A Little Night Music;* Director: *Follies, Sweeny Todd.* New York Drama Critics Awards (Producer)—*Fiorello, Fiddler On The Roof, Cabaret, Company, Follies, A Little Night Music, Candide.* Pulitzer Prize — *Fiorello.*

JOSE QUINTERO, *Director*
Born: October 15, 1924;
        Panama City, Panama

Theatre Companies: Circle In The Square — co-founder; directed *Dark Of The Moon,* 1950; *The Bonds Of Interest,* 1951; *The Enchanted,* 1951; *Yerma,* 1951; *Burning Bright,* 1951; *Summer And Smoke,* 1952; *The Grass Harp,* 1953; *The Girl On The Via Flaminia,* 1954; *La Ronde,* 1955; *Cradle Song,* 1955; *The Iceman Cometh* (also co-producer), 1956; *Children Of Darkness,* 1958; *The Quare Fellow,* 1958; *Our Town,* 1959; *The Balcony,* 1960; *Under Milkwood* (co-producer), 1961; *Plays For Bleecker Street,* 1962. Actor's Studio — *Strange Interlude,* 1963. Repertory Theatre Of Lincoln Center—

Marco Millions, 1964. Buffalo Studio Arena—*A Moon For The Misbegotten,* 1965; *Episode In The Life Of An Author* and *The Orchestra,* 1969; *Gabrielle* (also author), 1974.

Broadway: *In The Summer House,* 1953; *Portrait Of A Lady,* 1954; *The Innkeepers,* 1956; *Long Day's Journey Into Night* (also co-producer), 1956; *Look, We've Come Through,* 1961; *Great Day In The Morning,* 1962; *Hughie,* 1964; *Diamond Orchid,* 1965; *Pousse-cafe,* 1966; *More Stately Mansions,* 1967; *The Seven Descents Of Myrtle,* 1968; *Gandhi,* 1970; *Johnny Johnson,* 1971; *A Moon For The Misbegotten,* 1973; *The Skin Of Our Teeth,* 1975; *Anna Christie,* 1977; *A Touch Of The Poet,* 1977; *The Faith Healer,* 1979.

Also: directed *Camino Real* (Off-Broadway) 1960, four works for the Metropolitan Opera, *The Roman Spring Of Mrs. Stone* (film) and numerous television dramas; author of *If You Don't Dance, They Beat You* (autobiography).

Awards: Vernon Rice Award — *The Iceman Cometh;* Tony Awards—*Long Day's Journey Into Night, A Moon For The Misbegotten;* Drama Desk Award — *The Moon For The Misbegotten.*

ELLIS RABB, *Actor/Director*
Born: June 20, 1930; Memphis, Tennessee

Association Of Producing Artists: Founder, 1960 and Artistic Director; directed *School For Scandal,* 1962; *The Tavern,* 1962; *The Sea Gull,* 1962; for A.P.A. at The Phoenix appeared in *Man And Superman,* 1964; *The Tavern,* 1964; *Scapin,* 1964; directed *The Lower Depths,* 1964; *War And Peace,* 1965; *Judith,* 1965; for A.P.A. — Phoenix directed *You Can't Take It With You,* 1965; *School For Scandal,* 1966; *We Comrades Three,* 1966; *War And Peace,* 1967; *Pantagleize* (co-director, also title role), 1967; *Exit The King,* 1968; *Hamlet* (also title role), 1969; appeared in *Cock-A-Doodle Dandy,* 1969.

Actor: appeared on Broadway in *Look After Lulu,* 1959; *Jolly's Progress,* 1959; *The Royal Family,* 1975; appeared Off-Broadway in *A Midsummer Night's Dream,* 1956; *The Misanthrope,* 1956; *Hamlet,* 1957; *Two Philoctetes,* 1959; *A Life In The Theatre,* 1977; appeared with the Phoenix Theatre in *Measure For Measure,* 1957; *The Duchess Of Malfi,* 1957; *Mary Stuart,* 1957; appeared with the American Shakespeare Festival in *Much Ado About Nothing,* 1957; *A Winter's Tale,* 1958; *Hamlet,*

1958; *A Midsummer Night's Dream*, 1958.
Director: Broadway — *The Glass Harp*, 1971; *Veronica's Room*, 1973; *Who's Who In Hell*, 1974; *Edward II*, 1975; *Caesar And Cleopatra*, 1977. San Diego Shakespeare Festival — various productions, 1963, 1968, 1969 and 1971. American Conservatory Theatre — various productions, 1970-72. Repertory Theatre Of Lincoln Center — *Twelfth Night*, 1972; *Enemies*, 1972; *The Merchant Of Venice*, 1973; *A Streetcar Named Desire* (also Broadway), 1973. McCarter Theatre — Guest Director, 1975-76. Brooklyn Academy Of Music — *The Royal Family (also Broadway)*, 1975.
Awards: Tony Award — *The Royal Family* (director); Obie Award — 1962-63 A.P.A. season; Clarence Derwent Award — *The Misanthrope*.

DAVID RABE, *Playwright*
Born: March 10, 1940; Dubuque, Iowa
Theatre Companies: New York Shakespeare Festival — *The Basic Training Of Pavlo Hummel*, 1971; *Sticks And Bones*, 1971 (also Broadway, 1972); *The Orphan*, 1973; *Boom Boom Room* (Lincoln Center), 1973 (revised as *In The Boom Boom Room* and presented at Public Theatre, 1974); *Burning*, 1974; *Streamers* (also at Long Wharf Theatre), 1976.
Awards: Obie and Drama Desk Awards — *The Basic Training Of Pavlo Hummel;* Tony Award and New York Drama Critics Citation — *Sticks And Bones;* New York Drama Critics Award — *Streamers.*

LYNN REDGRAVE, *Actor*
Born: March 8, 1943; London, England
Theatre Companies: Royal Court — *A Midsummer Night's Dream*, 1962; *Slag*, 1971. National Theatre Of Great Britain — various roles, 1963-66; New York Shakespeare Festival — *Mrs. Warren's Profession* (Lincoln Center), 1976.
Broadway: *Black Comedy*, 1967; *My Fat Friend*, 1974.
Great Britain: *Zoo Zoo Widdershins* (Edinburgh), 1969; *The Two Of Us* (London), 1970; *A Better Place* (Dublin), 1972; *Born Yesterday* (London), 1973.
Also: various films including *Tom Jones, Girl With Green Eyes* and *Georgy Girl* and television appearances.

VANESSA REDGRAVE, *Actor*
Born: January 30, 1937; London, England
England: *The Reluctant Debutante*, 1957; *A Touch Of The Sun*, 1957; *Major Barbara* (Royal Court), 1958; *Othello, A Midsummer Night's Dream and Coriolanus* (Royal Shakespeare Company), 1959; *Look On Tempests*, 1960; *Lady From The Sea*, 1960; *The Taming Of The Shrew*, 1961 and *As You Like It*, 1962 (Royal Shakespeare Company); *The Sea Gull*, 1964; *The Prime Of Miss Jean Brodie*, 1966; *Daniel Deronda*, 1969; *Cato Street* (Young Vic), 1971; *Threepenny Opera*, 1972; *Twelfth Night*, 1972; *Antony And Cleopatra*, 1973.
New York: *Design For Living* (Phoenix Theatre), 1973; *Lady From The Sea* (Circle In The Square), 1976.
Also: films include *Blow Up, A Man For All Seasons, Camelot, Isadora, Mary Queen Of Scots, Murder On The Orient Express, Agatha, Bear Island.*

ANN REINKING, *Actor*
Born: November 10, 1949; Seattle, Washington
Broadway: *Cabaret*, 1969; *Coco*, 1969; *Pippin*, 1972; *Over Here*, 1974; *Goodtime Charley*, 1975; *A Chorus Line*, 1976; *Chicago*, 1977; *Dancin'*, 1978.
Awards: Clarence Derwent Award — *Over Here;* Drama Desk Award — *Goodtime Charley.*

JASON ROBARDS, *Actor*
Born: July 26, 1922; Chicago, Illinois
Theatre Companies: Circle In The Square — *American Gothic*, 1953; *The Iceman Cometh*, 1956. Stratford (Ontario) Shakespeare Festival — *Henry IV, The Winter's Tale*, 1958; Repertory Theatre Of Lincoln Center — *After The Fall*, 1964; *But For Whom Charlie*, 1964. Brooklyn Academy Of Music — *Long Day's Journey Into Night*, 1976.
Broadway: *Long Day's Journey Into Night*, 1956; *The Disenchanted*, 1958; *Toys In The Attic*, 1960; *Big Fish, Little Fish*, 1961; *A Thousand Clowns*, 1962; *Hughie*, 1964; *The Devils*, 1965; *We Bombed In New Haven*, 1968; *The Country Girl*, 1972; *A Moon For The Misbegotten*, 1973; *A Touch Of The Poet*, 1977.
Also: films include *By Love Possessed, Tender Is The Night, Long Day's Journey Into*

Night, A Thousand Clowns, Any Wednesday, The Ballad Of Cable Hogue, All The President's Men, Comes A Horseman, Julia, Hurricane.
Awards: Tony Award — *The Disenchanted, Touch Of The Poet;* Obie Award — *The Iceman Cometh;* New York Drama Critics Award — *Long Day's Journey Into Night;* Academy (Oscar) Award—*All The President's Men.*

JEROME ROBBINS, *Director/ Choreographer*
Born: October 11, 1918; New York, New York
Choreographer: *On The Town,* 1944; *Interplay,* 1945; *Billion Dollar Baby,* 1945; *Miss Liberty,* 1949; *The King And I,* 1951; *Wonderful Town,* 1953; *Two's Company,* 1951.
Director/Choreographer: *High Button Shoes,* 1947; *Look Ma, I'm Dancin'* (co-director, also author), 1948; *Call Me Madam,* 1950; *Peter Pan* (also adapted), 1954; *The Bells Are Ringing,* 1956; *West Side Story* (also conceived), 1957; *Gypsy,* 1959; *Fiddler On The Roof,* 1964.
Director: *The Pajama Game* (co-director), 1954; *Oh Dad, Poor Dad, Mama's Hung You In The Closet And I'm Feelin' So Sad,* 1962; *Mother Courage,* 1963.
Also: New York City Ballet — joined, 1949; named Associate Artistic Director, 1950; choreographed numerous works. Formed Ballet: U.S.A., 1958. Choreographed for Ballet Theatre, American Ballet Theatre, Joffrey Ballet, Harkness Ballet, Royal Ballet. Choreographed the films *The King And I* and *West Side Story* (also co-director).
Awards: Tony Awards—*High Button Shoes, West Side Story;* Donaldson Awards—*Billion Dollar Baby, High Button Shoes, The King And I, Two's Company, The Pajama Game;* Academy (Oscar) Award — *West Side Story.* New York Drama Critics Award—*Fiddler On The Roof.*

RICHARD RODGERS, *Composer/ Producer*
Born: June 28, 1902; New York, New York
Composer, with Lorenz Hart as Lyricist: twenty-eight stage musicals including *Poor Little Ritz Girl,* 1920; *The Garrick Gaieties,* 1925; *Dearest Enemy,* 1925; *Lido Lady* (London), 1926; *The Girl Friend,* 1926; *Peggy-Ann,* 1926; *One Damn Thing After Another* (London), 1927; *A Connecticut Yankee,* 1927; *Present Arms,* 1928; *Spring Is Here,* 1929; *Heads Up,* 1929; *Ever Green* (London), 1930; *America's Sweetheart,* 1931; *Jumbo,* 1935; *On Your Toes* (also co-author), 1936; *Babes In Arms* (also co-author), 1937; *I'd Rather Be Right,* 1937; *I Married An Angel* (also co-author), 1938; *The Boys From Syracuse,* 1938; *Too Many Girls,* 1939; *Higher And Higher,* 1940; *Pal Joey,* 1940; *By Jupiter* (also co-author), 1942.
Composer, with Oscar Hammerstein, II as Lyricist: *Oklahoma,* 1943; *Carousel,* 1945; *Allegro,* 1947; *South Pacific* (also co-producer), 1949; *The King And I* (also co-producer), 1951; *Me And Juliet,* 1953; *Pipe Dream,* 1955; *Flower Drum Song* (also co-producer), 1958; *The Sound Of Music* (also co-producer), 1959.
Composer, with other Lyricists: *No Strings* (also lyricist and producer), 1962; *Do I Hear A Waltz* (lyrics by Stephen Sondheim, also producer), 1965; *Two By Two* (lyrics by Martin Charnin, also producer), 1970; *Rex* (lyrics by Sheldon Harnick, also producer), 1976; *I Remember Mama* (lyrics by Martin Charnin), 1979.
Co-Producer: *I Remember Mama,* 1944; *Annie Get Your Gun,* 1946; *Happy Birthday,* 1946; *John Loves Mary,* 1947; *The Happy Time,* 1950; *Burning Bright,* 1950; *Avanti,* 1968; President and Producing Director, Music Theatre Of Lincoln Center, 1964-69.
Also: films include *Hallelujah I'm A Bum, Love Me Tonight* and *Mississippi* with Hart and *State Fair* with Hammerstein in addition to film adaptations of thirteen stage musicals with Hart and six with Hammerstein; television scores include *Victory At Sea, Cinderella* and *Winston Churchill—The Valiant Years;* author of *Musical Stages* (autobiography).
Awards: Pulitzer Prizes—*Oklahoma* (special award), *South Pacific;* Tony Awards—*South Pacific, The King And I, No Strings,* Special Tonys 1962, 1979; New York Drama Critics Awards — *Carousel, South Pacific, Pal Joey;* Donaldson Awards—*Carousel, Allegro, South Pacific, Pal Joey;* Academy (Oscar) Awards—*"It Might As Well Be Spring"* (from *State Fair*), *The Sound Of Music;* elected to National Institute Of Arts And Letters.

VINCENT SARDI, *Restaurateur*
Born: July 23, 1915; New York, New York
Sardi's Restaurant: Owner-Manager

Also: Chairman, *Restaurant League Of New York;* Member Board Of Directors, *New York State Restaurant Association, The Broadway Association, New York Convention And Visitors Bureau;* Member Food Trades Educational Advisory Commission, New York Board Of Education, Mayor's Midtown Citizens Committee; various television and radio appearances.

ALAN SCHNEIDER, *Director*
Born: December 12, 1917; Kharkov, Russia

Theatre Companies: Arena Stage—Artistic Director, 1952-53; Associate Director, 1961-63, 1971-70; directed numerous productions including premieres of *All Summer Long* (also Broadway), 1953; *The Bad Angel,* 1953; *A View From The Bridge,* 1956; *Clandestine On The Morning Line,* 1959; *The Caucasian Chalk Circle,* 1961; *The Burning Of The Lepers,* 1962; *Moonchildren* (also Broadway), 1971; *Uptight,* 1972; *The Foursome,* 1972; *Tom,* 1973; *Zalmen, Or The Madness Of God* (also Broadway), 1974. Alley Theatre—*Waiting For Godot,* 1959. New York Shakespeare Festival — *Measure For Measure,* 1960. Goodman Theatre — *Uncle Vanya,* 1961. Guthrie Theatre — *The Glass Menagerie,* 1964. Buffalo Studio Arena—*Box-Mao-Box* (also Broadway), 1968; *Krapp's Last Tape* and *The Zoo Story,* 1968. The Acting Company—Artistic Director, 197 -7 ; directed *Mother Courage,* 197 and *Antigone,* 1979.
Broadway: *A Long Way From Home,* 1948; *The Remarkable Mr. Pennypacker,* 1953; *Anastasia,* 1954; *Tonight In Samarkand,* 1955; *The Skin Of Our Teeth,* 1955; *The Little Glass Clock,* 1956; *Miss Lonelyhearts,* 1957; *Who's Afraid Of Virginia Woolf?,* 1962; *The Ballad Of The Sad Cafe,* 1963; *Tiny Alice,* 1964; *Entertaining Mr. Sloane,* 1965; *Malcolm,* 1966; *Slapstick Tragedy,* 1966; *You Know I Can't Hear You When The Water's Running,* 1967; *A Delicate Balance,* 1967; *The Birthday Party,* 1967; *I Never Sang For My Father,* 1968; *The Watering Place,* 1969; *The Gingham Dog,* 1969; *La Strada,* 1969; *Blood Red Roses,* 1970; *Inquest,* 1970; *The Sign In Sidney Brustein's Window,* 1972; *A Texas Trilogy,* 197?.
Off-Broadway: *Pullman Car Hiawatha,* 1952; *Hide And Seek,* 1953; *Endgame,* 1958 and 1962; *Krapp's Last Tape,* 1960 and 1965; *The American Dream,* 1961 and 1964; *Happy Days,* 1961, 1962 and 1965; *The Dumbwaiter*

and *The Collection,* 1962; *Play* and *The Lover,* 1964; *Do Not Pass Go,* 1965; *The Zoo Story,* 1965; *Waiting For Godot,* 1971.
Also: *Waiting For Godot* (American Premiere, Coconut Grove Playhouse), 1956; directed the film of Samuel Beckett's, *Film;* Drama Critic of *the New Leader,* 1962-63.
Awards: Tony Award — *Who's Afraid Of Virginia Woolf?;* Obie Award — *The Dumbwaiter* and *The Collection.*

GERALD SCHOENFELD, *Theatre Owner/Producer*
Born: September 22, 1924;
       New York, New York

The Shubert Organization: Chairman Of The Board, since 1972, of this theatrical organization which owns and operates seventeen theatres in New York, two in Chicago and one each in Boston, Philadelphia and Los Angeles; *The Shubert Organization* has also co-produced *Sherlock Holmes,* 1975; *Sly Fox,* 1976; *Fiddler On The Roof,* 1976; *The Act,* 1977; *The Gin Game,* 1977; *Ain't Misbehavin',* 1978; *Richard III,* 1979.
Also: Member Of The Board Of Governors, League Of New York Theatres And Producers, Inc; Member Of The Boards of 42nd Street Local Development Corp, New York City Convention And Visitors Bureau, The Broadway Association; Chairman, Mayor's Citizens Committee (New York) and member Mayor's Task Force On Urban Theatres (Boston).

ANDREI SERBAN, *Director*
Born: June 21, 1943; Bucharest, Romania

Theatre Companies: La Mama, ETC — *Arden Of Faversham,* 1970; *Ubu Roi,* 1970 and in collaboration with Elizabeth Swados *Medea,* 1972; *Electra,* 1973; *The Trojan Women,* 1974; *Good Woman Of Setzuan,* 1975; *As You Like It,* 1976. American Conservatory Theatre — 1974-75 season; New York Shakespeare Festival—*The Cherry Orchard,* 1977; *Agamemnon,* 1977; *The Master And Margarida,* 1978; *The Umbrellas Of Cherbourg,* 1979. Yale Repertory Theatre — *The Ghost Sonata, Sganarelle,* 1978; Member Of Peter Brook's International Center Of Theatrical Research.
Also: La Mama productions above performed in 13 countries at over 50 international festivals and *As You Like It* performed in Brittany, France.

Awards: Obie Award — Special Citation, 1975.

ROBERT SHAW, *Actor/Playwright*
Born: August 9, 1927; Westhoughton, Lancastershire, England (Died: 1979)
Theatre Companies: Shakespeare Memorial Theatre — various roles, 1949-50 and 1952-53; Old Vic Company — *Othello, A Midsummer Night's Dream,* 1951-52; New Shakespeare Theatre (in *One More River*), 1958; Royal Court (in *Live Like Pigs*), 1958; New York Shakespeare Festival (in *The Dance Of Death,* at Lincoln Center), 1974.
London: *Hamlet,* 1951; *Antony And Cleopatra,* 1953; *Tiger At The Gates,* 1955; *Off The Mainland,* 1956; *Shadow Of Heroes,* 1958; *The Long And The Short And The Tall,* 1959; *A Lodging For A Bride,* 1960; *The Changeling,* 1961.
Broadway: *The Caretaker,* 1961; *The Physicists,* 1964; *Gantry,* 1970; *Old Times,* 1971.
Author: *Off The Mainland* (1956), *The Man In The Glass Booth* (1967), *Cato Street* (1971) and the novels *The Hiding Place, The Sun Doctor, The Flag, The Man In The Glass Booth, A Card From Morocco.*

MARTIN SHEEN, *Actor*
Born: August 3, 1940; Dayton, Ohio
Theatre Companies: The Living Theatre — *The Connection,* 1959; *Women Of Trachis,* 1960; *Many Loves,* 1960; *In The Jungle Of Cities,* 1961. New York Shakespeare Festival — *Hamlet,* 1967; *Romeo And Juliet,* 1968; *The Happiness Cage,* 1970. Circle In The Square — *Death Of A Salesman,* 1975.
Off-Broadway: *The Wicked Cooks,* 1967; *Hello And Goodby,* 1969.
Broadway: *The Subject Was Roses,* 1964; *Never Live Over A Pretzel Factory,* 1964.
Also: wrote (as Ramon G. Estevez) *Down The Morning Line* (New York Shakespeare Festival), 1969; various films including *The Subject Was Roses, Catch 22* and *Badlands;* numerous television appearances including *The Andersonville Trials, That Certain Summer* and *The Execution Of Private Slovik.*

EDWIN SHERIN, *Director*
Born: Danville, Pennsylvania
Theatre Companies: Equity Library Theatre — *Joan Of Lorraine* and *Mister Roberts,* 1960. Arena Stage — Producing Director, 1964-69;

staged over fifteen productions including *The Great White Hope* (also Broadway, 1968). American Conservatory Theatre—*Glory! Hallelujah!,* 1969; Mark Taper Forum — *The Pastime Of Monsieur Robert,* 1970. American Shakespeare Theatre—*Major Barbara,* 1972. American Place Theatre—*Baba Goya,* 1973. New York Shakespeare Festival—*King Lear,* 1973. Brooklyn Academy Of Music—*Sweet Bird Of Youth,* (also Broadway) 1975. Buffalo Studio Arena—*Eccentricities Of A Nightingale* (also Broadway), 1976; *Semmelweiss,* 1978.
Broadway: *6 Rms Riv Vu,* 1972; *An Evening With Richard Nixon And...,* 1972; *Find Your Way Home,* 1974; *Of Mice And Men,* 1975; *Rex,* 1976; *Do You Turn Somersaults,* 1977.
Also: *Diedre Of The Sorrows* (Off-Broadway), 1959; *The Time Of Your Life* (Kennedy Center), 1972; *A Streetcar Named Desire* (London), 1974.
Actor: appeared with the New York Shakespeare Festival, 1957-58; the Phoenix Theatre, 1957, 1960; Off-Broadway in *Dr. Willy Nilly,* 1959, *Dif'rent,* 1961 and *Night Of The Auk,* 1963; over seventy-five television dramas.
Awards: Drama Desk Award — *The Great White Hope.*

SYLVIA SIDNEY, *Actor*
born: August 10, 1910, Bronx, New York
Broadway: *The Squall,* 1926; *Gods Of The Lightning,* 1928; *Nice Women,* 1929; *Cross Roads,* 1929; *Many A Slip,* 1930; *Bad Girl,* 1930; *To Quito And Back,* 1937; *The Fourposter,* 1952; *A Very Special Baby,* 1956; *Enter Laughing,* 1963; *Barefoot In The Park,* 1963.
Tours: *Pygmalion,* 1938, 1942-43, 1949; *Tonight At 8:30,* 1938; *Accent On Youth,* 1941; *Angel Street,* 1942; *Jane Eyre,* 1943; *Joan Of Lorraine,* 1947; *Kind Lady,* 1948, 1964; *O Mistress Mine,* 1948; *The Two Mrs. Carrolls,* 1949; *Good Bye Mr. Fancy,* 1950; *Anne Of The Thousand Days,* 1950; *The Innocents,* 1950; *Auntie Mame,* 1959; *Angel Street,* 1964; *The Silver Cord,* 1964; *Barefoot In The Park,* 1966; *Come Blow Your Horn,* 1968.
Theatre Companies: The Group Theatre — *The Gentle People,* 1939; National Repertory Theatre—*The Rivals,* 1966; *The Madwoman Of Chaillot,* 1966; *She Stoops To Conquer,* 1968. Oakland Repertory Theatre — *The Importance Of Being Earnest,* 1967; Seattle

Repertory Theatre—*A Family And A Fortune*, 1974.
Also: numerous films from *Through Different Eyes*, 1920 to *Summer Wishes, Winter Dreams*, 1973 and television appearances.

STANLEY SILVERMAN, *Composer*
Born: July 5, 1938; Bronx, New York
Theatre Companies: Repertory Theatre Of Lincoln Center — Musical Director and composer of incidental music for *The Country Wife*, 1965; *Yerman*, 1966; *Galileo*, 1967; *St. Joan*, 1968; *Tiger At The Gates*, 1968; *Beggar On Horseback*, 1970; *Mary Stuart*, 1971; *Narrow Road To The Deep North*, 1972. Guthrie Theatre — Music Consultant and composer of incidental music for *The Taming Of the Shrew*, 1971; *Oedipus*, 1972; Stratford (Ontario) Shakespeare Festival — Music Consultant and composer of incidental music for *Richard III*, 1967; *A Midsummer Night's Dream*, 1968; *Satyricon*, 1969; *School For Scandal*, 1970; New York Shakespeare Festival — Music Director, *Threepenny Opera* (conducting debut), 1976; composer of incidental music for *Julius Caesar* and *Coriolanus*, 1979. Mark Taper Forum — incidental music for *The Tempest*, 1979.
Music-Theatre Pieces: *Elephant Steps* (Berkshire Music Festival, 1968 and Hunter College Opera Theatre, 1970); *Dream Tantras For Western Massachussets* (Lenox Arts Center), 1971; *Dr. Selavy's Magic Theatre* (Lenox Arts Center and Off-Broadway), 1972; *Hotel For Criminals* (Lenox Arts Center, 1974 and Off-Broadway, 1975); *The American Imagination* (Music Theatre Performing Group), 1978.
Also: composed scores for the films *Nanook Of The North, Strong Medecine and Simon*; various other orchestral, chamber music and vocal compositions.
Awards: Obie Award — *Elephant Steps*; Drama Desk Award—

NEIL SIMON, *Playwright*
Born: July 4, 1927; Bronx, New York
Broadway: *Come Blow Your Horn*, 1961; *Little Me*, 1962; *Barefoot In The Park*, 1963; *The Odd Couple*, 1965; *Sweet Charity*, 1966; *The Star Spangled Girl*, 1966; *Promises, Promises*, 1968; *Plaza Suite*, 1968; *The Last Of The Red Hot Lovers*, 1969; *The Gingerbread Lady*, 1970; *The Prisoner Of Second*

Avenue, 1971; *The Sunshine Boys*, 1972; *The Good Doctor*, 1973; *God's Favorite*, 1974; *California Suite*, 1976; *Chapter Two*, 1977; *They're Playing Our Song*, 1979.
Also: wrote screenplays for various films based on his plays as well as *The Out Of Towners, Murder By Death, After The Fox* and *The Heartbreak Kid*; television writer for *The Sid Caesar Show, The Gary Moore Show* and *The Phil Silvers Show*.
Awards: Tony Awards — *The Odd Couple*, "over-all contribution to the theatre", 1975; Writers Guild Award—*The Odd Couple*.

ISAAC BASHEVIS SINGER *Writer*
Born: July 14, 1904; Radzymin, Poland
Plays: *Devils Game* (Isidor Straus Theatre Alliance), 1959; *The Mirror* (Yale Repertory Theatre), 1973; *Shlemiel The First* (Yale Repertory Theatre), 1974; *Yentl The Yeshiva Boy* (Chelsea Theatre Center, also Broadway), 1974.
Also: *Satan In Goray, The Family Moskat, Gimpel The Fool, The Magician Of Lublin, The Spinoza Of Market Street, The Slave, Short Friday, In My Father's Court, The Manor, The Seance, The Estate, Enemies—A Love Story, Hassidim, The Fools Of Chelm And Their History, A Crown Of Feathers, Why Noah Chose The Dove* and *Shosha*.
Awards: National Book Awards — 1970, 1974; Nobel Prize In Literature, 1978.

JOHN SPRINGER, *Theatrical Public Relations*
Born: Rochester, New York
Public Relations: President, John Springer Associates, Inc., whose clients include *Richard Burton, Henry Fonda, Bonnie Franklin, Robert Preston, Harold Prince, Tony Randall, Elizabeth Taylor, Liv Ullmann*; past clients include *Montgomery Clift, Marlene Dietrich, Judy Garland, Marilyn Monroe, Mary Pickford*.
Author: as film historian books include *All Talking! All Singing! All Dancing!, Love For Sale, The Fondas, They Had Faces Then*.
Also: originated *Tribute Evenings* featuring *Bette Davis, Joan Crawford, Myrna Loy, Debbie Reynolds, Rosalind Russell, Sylvia Sidney, Lana Turner, Joanne Woodward*.

MAUREEN STAPLETON, *Actor*
Born: June 21, 1925; Troy, New York
Broadway: *Playboy Of The Western World,*

1946; *Antony And Cleopatra*, 1947; *The Detective Story*, 1949; *The Bird Cage*, 1950;*The Rose Tattoo*, 1951; *The Emperor's Clothes*, 1953; *The Crucible*, 1953; *27 Wagons Full Of Cotton*, 1955; *Orpheus Descending*, 1957; *Cold Wind And The Warm*, 1958; *Toys In The Attic*, 1960; *The Glass Menagerie*, 1965; *Plaza Suite*, 1968; *Norman Is That You?*, 1970; *The Gingerbread Lady*, 1970; *The Country Girl*, 1972; *The Secret Affairs Of Mildred Wild*, 1972; *The Gin Game*, 1978.

Theatre Companies: *Richard III*, 1953 and *The Rose Tattoo*, 1966 (NY City Center); *The Seagull* (Phoenix Theatre), 1954; *Juno And The Paycock* (Mark Taper Forum), 1974; *The Glass Menagerie* (Circle In The Square), 1975.

Also: various films including *The Fugitive Kind*, *A View From The Bridge*, *Bye Bye Birdie*, *Plaza Suite* and *Interiors;* numerous television appearances including *Goodyear Playhouse, Philco Playhouse, Armstrong Circle Theatre, Kraft Theatre, Playhouse 90, East Side /West Side, Among The Paths To Eden,* and *Queen Of The Stardust Ballroom.*

Awards: Tony Awards — *The Rose Tattoo, The Gingerbread Lady;* Peabody Award — *The Rose Tattoo;* Drama Desk Award — *The Gingerbread Lady;* Emmy Award — *Among The Paths To Eden;* National Institute Of Arts and Letters Award—1969.

ELLEN STEWART, *Producer (Founder, Executive Director La Mama Experimental Theatre Club)*
Born: Alexandra, Louisiana

Productions: since 1962 over 500 plays by approximately 200 playwrights including *One Arm*, 1962; *In A Corner Of The Morning*, 1962; *The Room*, 1962; *The Rimers Of Eldritch*, 1966; *Futz*, 1967; *Tom Paine*, 1967; *The Unseen Hand*, 1969; *A Rat's Mass*, 1971; *Fragments Of A Trilogy*, 1975.

Playwrights: playwrights produced at La Mama include *Harold Pinter, Paul Foster, Leonard Melfi, Lanford Wilson, Israel Horovitz, Tom Eyen, Sam Shepard, Megan Terry, Jean-Claude van Itallie, Rochelle Owens, Adrienne Kennedy, Charles Ludlam.*

Directors: directors who have worked frequently at La Mama include *John Braswell, Julie Bovasso, Wilford Leach, Tom O'Horgan, John Vaccaro, Ed Setrakian, Andrei Serban, Joel Zwick.*

Also: since 1970 La Mama has increasingly emphasized the presentation of works by experimental theatre groups and has provided a base of operations for *Play-House Of The Ridiculous, Jarboro Company, Native American Theatre Ensemble, Third World Institute Of The Arts!* La Mama troupes have played in major theatres and festivals all over the world including those in Berlin, Vienna, Rome, Spoleto, Paris, Venice, Brussels, Copenhagen, Zurich, Madrid, Barcelona, Dubrovnik, Shiraz, Belgrade, Bogota, Caen, Baalbeck, Amsterdam, Rotterdam, Helsinki and Avignon.

Awards: Margo Jones Award, New York State Award and Special Obie Award to Ellen Stewart; Special Obie Citations to La Mama, 1965, 1967; Obie Award—*Futz.*

LEE STRASBERG, *Actor/Director/Teacher*
Born: November 17, 1901;
      Budanov, Austria-Hungary

Theatre Companies: Group Theatre — Co-Founder and member, 1931-37; co-directed *The House Of Connelly*, 1931; director *Night Over Taos, Success Story, Gentlewoman, Gold, The Case Of Clyde Griffiths, Johnny Johnson, Many Mansions.* Actors' Studio — member, since 1947; Director, since 1948; directed *The Three Sisters* (Broadway), 1964.

Broadway: appeared in *The Four Walls*, 1927; *Red Rust*, 1929; *Green Grow The Lilacs*, 1931; directed *Hilda Cassiday*, 1933; *Roosty*, 1938; *All The Living*, 1938; *Dance Night*, 1938; *Summer Night*, 1939; *The Fifth Column*, 1940; *Clash By Night*, 1941; *R.U.R.*, 1942; *Apology* (also Producer), 1943; *South Pacific* (drama), 1943; *The Big Knife,* 1949; *Closing Door,* 1949; *Peer Gynt*, 1951.

Also: teaches acting at the Lee Strasberg Theatre Institute; appeared in the film *The Godfather, Part II.*

MERYL STREEP, *Actor*
Born: Bernardsville, New Jersey

Theatre Companies: Yale Repertory Theatre — member, 1974-75 season; New York Shakespeare Festival—*Trelawny Of The Wells*, 1975; *Measure For Measure*, 1976; *Henry V*, 1976; *The Cherry Orchard*, 1977; *The Taming Of The Shrew*, 1978; *Taken In Marriage*, 1979. Phoenix Theatre — *27 Wagons Full Of Cotton, A Memory Of Two Mondays, Secret Service*, 1976.

Also: *Happy End* (Broadway), 1977; films include Julia, The Deer Hunter, Kramer Vs.

Kramer, Manhattan; appeared on television in *Holocaust.*
Awards: Outer Circle Critics Award — *27 Wagons Full Of Cotton.* Obie Award—*Taken In Marriage.*

ELIZABETH SWADOS, *Author/Composer/Director*
Born: February 5, 1951; Buffalo, New York
Theatre Companies: La Mama, ETC — collaborated with Andrei Serban and composed the music for *Medea,* 1972; *Electra,* 1973; *The Trojan Women,* 1974; *Fragments Of A Trilogy,* 1975; *The Good Woman Of Setzuan,* 1975. New York Shakespeare Festival—*The Cherry Orchard* (composer), 1977; *Agamemnon* (collaborated with Serban and composed music), 1977; *Runaways* (author/composer/director), 1978; *Dispatches* (adaptor/composer/director), 1979. Member of Peter Brook's International Center Of Theatrical Research.
Also: *Nightclub Cantata* (Off-Broadway; conceived/composed/directed); composed ballets for the National Theatre of Canada; various television and film scores including *Step By Step;* author of *The Girl With The Incredible Feeling* and *For All Our Children.*
Awards: Obie Awards — *Medea, Nightclub Cantata, Runaways.*

JESSICA TANDY, *Actor*
Born: June 7, 1902; London, England
Theatre Companies: various productions in England with the Brimingham Repertory Company, 1928; Cambridge Festival Theatre, 1932; The Old Vic, 1937, 1940. Actors Laboratory Theatre—*Portrait Of A Madonna,* 1946. Phoenix Theatre — *Madam Will You Walk,* 1953. American Shakespeare Festival—*Macbeth, Troilus And Cressida,* 1961. Guthrie Theatre — 1963 (first) season, 1965 season. Mark Taper Forum—*The Miser,* 1968. Shaw Festival (Ontario)—*Heartbreak House,* 1968. Repertory Theatre Of Lincoln Center — *Camino Real,* 1970; Samuel Beckett Festival, 1972. Stratford (Ontario) Shakespeare Festival—1976-77 season. Long Wharf Theatre—*The Gin Game* (also Broadway), 1977.
Broadway: *The Matriarch,* 1930; *The Last Enemy,* 1930; *The White Seed,* 1939; *Geneva,* 1940; *Jupiter Laughs,* 1940; *A Streetcar Named Desire,* 1947; *Hilda Crane,* 1950; *The Fourposter,* 1951; *The Honeys,*

1955; *A Day By The Sea,* 1955; *The Man In The Dog Suit,* 1958; *Triple Play,* 1959; *Five Finger Exercise,* 1959; *The Physicists,* 1964; *A Delicate Balance,* 1966; *Home,* 1970; *All Over,* 1971; *In Two Keys,* 1974.
Also: in addition to appearances with theatre companies, over thirty-five productions on the London stage; films include *The Seventh Cross, Valley Of Decision, Dragonwyck, Forever Amber, Adventures Of A Young Man, The Birds;* various television appearances.
Awards: Tony Award — *A Streetcar Named Desire, The Gin Game.* Obie and Drama Desk Awards—*Samuel Beckett Festival.*

LIV ULLMANN, *Actor*
Born: December 16, 1939; Tokyo, Japan
Theatre (Norway); *The Diary Of Anne Frank* (debut); numerous roles with the National and Norwegian Theatres including *Juliet, Ophelia* and *St. Joan.*
Theatre (US): *A Doll's House* (New York Shakespeare Festival at Lincoln Center), 1975; *Anna Christie* (Broadway), 1978; *I Remember Mama* (Broadway), 1979.
Also: appeared in the Ingmar Bergman films *Persona, Hour Of The Wolf, Shame, Cries And Whispers, Face To Face, Scenes From A Marriage, The Serpent's Egg, Autumn Sonata;* other films include *The Emigrants, The New Land, Lost Horizon, Forty Carats, The abdication;* author of the book *Changing.*
Awards: New York Film Critics Awards — *Cries And Whispers, Scenes From A Marriage;* Peer Gynt Award — from the Norwegian government.

JOHN VACCARO, *Director/Playwright/Actor*
Born: December 6, 1929; Steubenville, Ohio
Play-House Of The Ridiculous: co-founded as Ridiculous Theatre, with playwright Ronald Tavel, 1965; directed thrity-four plays, primarily musicals, many performed at La Mama, ETC and five of which toured extensively throughout Europe; author (also director) *Persia, A Desert Cheapie,* 1972 and *La Bohemia.*
Awards: Obie Award — Special Citation, 1970.

GWEN VERDON, *Actor*
Born: January 13, 1926;
      Culver City, California
Broadway: *Alive And Kicking,* 1950; *Can*

Can, 1953; *Damn Yankees*, 1955; *New Girl In Town*, 1957; *Redhead*, 1959; *Chicago*, 1975.
Also: Assistant Choreographer—*Magdalena*, 1948; *Alive And Kicking* and the film, *On The Riviera;* films include *Damn Yankees.*
Awards: Tony Awards — *Can Can, Damn Yankees, Redhead;* Donaldson Awards—*Can Can.*

ROBIN WAGNER, *Set and Lighting Designer*
Born: August 31, 1933;
        San Francisco, California
Off-Broadway: sets and lighting for *And The Wind Blows*, 1959; *The Prodigal*, 1960; *Between Two Thieves*, 1960; *Borak*, 1960; *A Worm In Horseradish*, 1961; *Entertain A Ghost*, 1962; *Days And Nights Of Beebee Fenstermaker*, 1962; *In White America*, 1963; *The Burning*, 1963; sets for *Cages*, 1963; *A Certain Young Man*, 1967; *Mahagony*, 1970.
Broadway: *The Trial Of Lee Harvey Oswald*, 1967; *Hair*, 1968; *The Cuban Thing*, 1968; *The Great White Hope*, 1968; *Lovers And Other Strangers*, 1968; *Promises, Promises*, 1968; *The Watering Place*, 1969; *My Daughter Your Son*, 1969; *Gantry*, 1970; *The Engagement Baby*, 1970; *Lenny*, 1971; *Jesus Christ Superstar*, 1971; *Inner City*, 1971; *Suga*, 1972; *Lysistrata*, 1972; *Seesaw*, 1973; *Full Circle*, 1973; *Mack And Mabel*, 1974; *A Chorus Line*, 1975; *On The Twentieth Century*, 1978.
Theatre Companies: Arena Stage — fourteen set designs as principal designer, 1964-67; *Edith Stein*, 1969. Repertory Theatre Of Lincoln Center—*The Condemned Of Altona*, 1966; *Galileo*, 1967; *In Three Zones*, 1968. American Shakespeare Festival — *Julius Caesar, Antony And Cleopatra*, 1972.
Also: various designs for for theatre, ballet and opera in San Francisco, 1953-59; conceived *Sgt. Pepper's Lonely Hearts Club Band On The Road*, 1974.
Awards: Tony Award — *On The Twentieth Century;* Drama Desk Award — *Lenny;* Majaram Award—*Seesaw.*

CHRISTOPHER WALKEN, *Actor*
Born: March 31, 1943; Astoria, New York
Theatre Companies: New York Shakespeare Festival—*Measure For Measure*, 1966; *Cymbeline*, 1971; *Troilus And Cressida*, 1973; *The Tempest*, 1974; *Macbeth*, 1974; *Kid Champion*. 1975. Circle In The Square—

Iphigenia In Aulis, 1967; Repertory Theatre Of Lincoln Center—*The Unknown Soldier And His Wife*, 1967; *Scenes From American Life*, 1971; *Enemies*, 1972; *The Plough And The Stars*, 1973; *The Merchant Of Venice*, 1973. American Shakespeare Theatre — *Romeo And Juliet, A Midsummer Night's Dream, The Three Musketeers*, 1968. San Diego Shakespeare Festival—*Comedy Of Errors* and *Julius Caesar*, 1969. Goodman Memorial Theatre—*The Night Thoreau Spent In Jail*, 1971. Yale Repertory Theatre — *Caligula*, 1971. American Place Theatre — *Metamorphosis*, 1972. Long Wharf Theatre — *Dance Of Death* and *Miss Julie*, 1973. Center Playhouse (Seattle) —*Hamlet*, 1974. Brooklyn Academy Of Music —*Sweet Bird Of Youth*, 1974.
Broadway: *J.B.*, 1958; *Best Foot Forward*, 1963; *High Spirits*, 1964; *Baker Street*, 1965; *The Lion In Winter*, 1966; *The Rose Tattoo* (City Center), 1966; *Lemon Sky*, 1970.
Also: films include *The Anderson Tapes, Next Stop Greenwich Village, Annie Hall* and *The Deer Hunter.*
Awards: Clarence Derwent Award — *The Lion In Winter;* Academy (Oscar) Award — *The Deer Hunter.*

ELI WALLACH, *Actor*
Born: December 7, 1915; Brooklyn, New York
Broadway: *Skydrift*, 1945; *Antony And Cleopatra*, 1947; *Mr. Roberts*, 1948; *The Rose Tattoo*, 1951; *Camino Real*, 1953; *Mlle. Colombe*, 1954; *Teahouse Of The August Moon*, 1953; *Major Barbara*, 1956; *The Cold Wind And The Warm*, 1958; *Rhinoceros*, 1961; *Luv* 1964; *Promenade All*, 1972.
Off-Broadway: *The Typists* and *The Tiger*, 1963; *The Diary Of Anne Frank*, 1979.
Theatre Companies: American Repertory Theatre—*Henry VIII* (also Broadway), 1946; *Yellow Jack*, 1947; *Alice In Wonderland*, 1947. Circle In The Square — *The Waltz Of The Toreadors*, 1973. Arena Stage — guest artist, 1977-78 season. Long Wharf Theatre—*Absent Friends*, 1977.
Also: various films and numerous television appearances.
Awards: Tony and Donaldson Awards—*The Rose Tattoo.*

TONY WALTON, *Set and Costume Designer*
Born: October 24, 1934;
        Walton-On-The-Thames,
        Surrey, England

Broadway: costumes: *The Rehearsal*, 1963; sets and costumes for Valmouth, 1960; *Once There Was A Russian*, 1961; *A Funny Thing Happened On The Way To The Forum*, 1962; *Golden Boy*, 1964; *The Apple Tree*, 1966; *The Good Doctor*, 1973, *Shelter*, 1973, sets for *Pippin*, 1972; *Chicago*, 1975.

Theatre Companies: designs for Wimbledon Repertory Company, 1955. National Theatre — sets and costumes for *Triple Bill*, 1968 and *The Travails Of Sancho Panza*, 1969. Circle In The Square — *Uncle Vanya*, 1973. New York Shakespeare Festival — *Streamers*, 1976; *Drinks Before Dinner*, 1978 (also Long Wharf Theatre).

London: various productions including *Valmouth*, 1958; *The Ginger Man*, 1959; *Pieces Of Eight*, 1959; *The Most Happy Fella*, 1960; *A Funny Thing ...*, 1963; *Caligula*, 1964; *Golden Boy*, 1968; *Pippin*, 1973.

Also: designs for the San Francisco Ballet, Santa Fe Opera Company, Sadler's Wells Theatre, Royal Opera; costume and production designs for the films *Mary Poppins*, *A Funny Thing...*, *Fahrenheit 451*, *Petulia*, *The Sea Gull*, *The Boy Friend*, *Murder On The Orient Express*, *Equus*, *The Wiz* and *Just Tell Me What You Want*. Design Consultant for *All That Jazz*. Illustrator of several books.

Awards: Tony Award—*Pippin;* Drama Desk Awards—*Pippin, Shelter*.

DOUGLAS TURNER WARD, *Actor /Director/Producer/Playwright*
Born: May 5, 1930; Burnside, Louisiana

Negro Ensemble Company: Co-Founder and Artistic Director since 1967. Appeared in *Kongi's Harvest*, 1968; *Daddy Goodness* (also director), 1968; *Ceremonies In Dark Old Men*, 1969; *The Harangues*, 1969; *Frederick Douglass*, 1972; *The River Niger* (also director), 1972 (also Broadway, 1973); *The First Breeze Of Summer* (also director; also Broadway), 1975; *The Brownsville Raid*, 1976; *The Offering* (also director), 1978; *Black Body Blues* (also director), 1978. Directed Contribution, 1969; *Man Better Man*, 1969; *Brotherhood* and *Day Of Absence*, 1970; *Perry's Mission*, 1971; *Ride A Black Horse*, 1971; *A Ballet Behind The Bridge*, 1972; *The Great Macdaddy*, 1974; *Waiting For Mongo*, 1975; *Livin' Fat*, 1976; *Twilight Dinner*, 1978.

Author: *Happy Ending*, 1965; *Day Of Absence*, 1965; *The Reckoning*, 1969; *Brotherhood*, 1970.

Actor: Broadway — *A Raisin In The Sun*, 1959; *One Flew Over The Cuckoo's Nest*, 1973. Off-Broadway—*The Blacks*, 1961; *The Blood Knot*, 1963; *Happy Ending* and *Day Of Absence*, 1965. *The Iceman Cometh*, 1956 and *Pullman Car Hiawatha*, 1962 (Circle In The Square); *Coriolanus* (New York Shakespeare Festival), 1965.

Also: various television appearances including *Ceremonies In Dark Old Men*.

Awards: Margo Jones Award — to Negro Ensemble Company, 1973; Obie Awards (actor) — *Day Of Absence, The River Niger;* Vernon Rice Award (author) — *Day Of Absence* and *Happy Ending*.

SAM WATERSTON, *Actor*
Born: November 15, 1940; Cambridge, Massachusetts

Broadway: *Oh Dad, Poor Dad, Mama's Hung You In The Closet And I'm Feeling So Sad*, 1963; *Halfway Up The Tree*, 1967; *Indians*, 1969; *Hay Fever*, 1970; *The Trial Of The Catonsville Nine*, 1971; *A Meeting By The River*, 1972.

Off-Broadway: *Thistle In My Bed*, 1963; *The Knack*, 1964; *Red Cross* and *Muzeeka*, 1968; *Spitting Image*, 1969.

Theatre Companies: Circle In The Square — *Fitz*, 1966. Cincinnati Playhouse In The Park—*Eh*, 1966. American Place Theatre— *La Tourista* and *Posterity For Sale*, 1967. New York Shakespeare Festival — *Ergo*, 1968; *Henry IV, Parts 1* and *2*, 1968; *Hamlet*, 1972; *Much Ado About Nothing* (also Broadway), 1972; *The Tempest*, 1974; *A Doll's House*, 1975; *Hamlet*, 1975. Chelsea Theatre Center — *The Brass Butterfly*, 1970. Mark Taper Forum — *Volpone*, 1971; *A Meeting By The River*, 1972.

Also: various film and television appearances.

Awards: Drama Desk, Drama Critics Circle and Obie Awards—*Much Ado About Nothing*.

MICHAEL WELLER, *Playwright*
Born: 1942; New York, New York

England: *How Soho Rose And Fell In Seven Short Scenes* (N.U.N. Festival), 1968; *The Making Of Theodore Thomas, Citizen* (Toynbee School Of Drama), 1968; *The Body Builders* (Open Space), 1969; *Cancer* (later titled *Moonchildren, Royal Court*), 1970.

United States: *Moonchildren* (Arena Stage, 1971, also Broadway, 1971 and Off-Broadway, 1973); *Now There's Just The Three Of Us* (Chelsea Theatre Center), 1971; *Twenty-Three Years Later* (Mark Taper Forum), 1973; *More Than You Deserve* (New York Shakespeare Festival), 1974; *Fishing* (New York Shakespeare Festival), 1975; *Lucky Joe And The Powers That Be*, 1975; *Loose Ends* (Circle In The Square), 1979.

ROBERT WHITEHEAD, *Producer*
Born: March 3, 1916; Montreal, Canada
Producer (Broadway): *Media*, 1947; *Crime And Punishment*, 1947; *The Member Of The Wedding*, 1950; *Tamburlaine The Great*, 1956; *Separate Tables*, 1956; *Major Barbara*, 1956; *The Sleeping Prince*, 1956; *The Day The Money Stopped*, 1958; *The Visit*, 1958; *A Touch Of The Poet*, 1958; *Goldilocks*, 1958; *The Cold Wind And The Warm*, 1958; *Much Ado About Nothing*, 1959. *The Time Of The Cuckoo*, 1952.
Co-Producer (Broadway): *Bus Stop*, 1955; *A View From The Bridge*, 1955; *The Conquering Hero*, 1961; *Midgie Purvis*, 1961; *A Man For All Seasons*, 1961; *The Prime Of Miss Jean Brodie*, 1968; *The Price*, 1968; *The Creation Of The World And Other Business*, 1972; *Finishing Touches*, 1973; *Bedroom Farce*, 1979.
Theatre Companies: ANTA—as Managing Director produced *Desire Under The Elms*, 1952; *Mrs. McThing*, 1952; *Golden Boy*, 1952; *Four Saints In Three Acts*, 1952; *Sunday Breakfast*, 1952. Producers Theatre—as Executive Producer co-produced *The Remarkable Mr. Pennypacker*, 1953; *The Confidential Clerk*, 1954; *The Flowering Peach*, 1954; *The Skin Of Our Teeth*, 1955; produced *The Emperor's Clothes*, 1953; *The Waltz Of The Toreadors*, 1957; *A Hole In The Head*, 1957; *Orpheus Descending*, 1957. Repertory Theatre Of Lincoln Center—as Co-Director co-produced *After The Fall*, 1964; *Marco Millions*, 1964; *But For Whom Charlie*, 1964; *The Changeling*, 1965; *Incident At Vichy*, 1965; *Tartuffe*, 1965.
Awards: New York Drama Critics Awards— *The Member Of The Wedding, The Waltz Of The Toreadors, The Visit, A Man For All Seasons.*

TENNESSEE WILLIAMS, *Playwright*
Born: May 26, 1911; Columbus, Mississippi

Early Plays: *Candles To The Sun*, 1936; *The Fugitive Kind*, 1937; *Spring Song*, 1938; *Not About Nightingales*, 1939; *Battle Of The Angels*, 1940; *Stairs To The Roof*, 1944.
Broadway: *The Glass Menagerie*, 1945; *You Touched Me* (co-author), 1945; *Summer And Smoke* (also Theatre '47, Dallas), 1947; *A Streetcar Named Desire*, 1947; *The Rose Tattoo*, 1951; *Camino Real*, 1953; *Cat On A Hot Tin Roof*, 1955; *27 Wagons Full Of Cotton*, 1955; *Orpheus Descending*, 1957; *This Property Is Condemned*, 1957; *Something Unspoken* and *Suddenly Last Summer*, 1958; *Sweet Bird Of Youth*, 1959; *Period Of Adjustment*, 1960; *The Night Of The Iguana*, 1961; *The Milktrain Doesn't Stop Here Anymore*, 1963; *Slapstick Tragedy*, 1966; *The Seven Descents Of Myrtle*, 1967; *Outcry* (previously titled *The Two Character Play*, London, 1967); *Vieux Carre*, 1977.
Also: (Actors Laboratory Theatre), *Portrait Of A Madonna*, 1946; *Three Players Of A Summer Game*, 1955 and *Talk To Me Like The Rain*, 1958 (White Barn Theatre, Westport); *I Rise In Flame Cried The Phoenix* (Phoenix Theatre), 1959; *The Purification* (ANTA Matinee Series), 1959; *The Red Devil Battery Sign* (Pre-Broadway), 1975.
Published Works (in addition to plays): *The Summer Belvedere, One Arm And Other Stories, The Roman Spring Of Mrs. Stone, Hard Candy, The Knightly Quest.*
Awards: Pulitzer Prizes—*A Streetcar Named Desire, Cat On A Hot Tin Roof;* Tony Award— *The Rose Tattoo;* New York Drama Critics Awards — *The Glass Menagerie, A Streetcar Named Desire, Cat On A Hot Tin Roof;* Donaldson Award — *The Streetcar Named Desire;* Gold Medal For Drama — National Institute Of Arts And Letters.

LANFORD WILSON, *Playwright*
Born: April 13, 1937; Lebanon, Missouri
Theatre Companies: Cafe Cino—*So Long At The Fair*, 1963; *Home Free* and *No Trespassing*, 1964; *The Madness Of Lady Bright*, 1964; *Ludlow Fair*, 1965; *This Is The Rill Speaking*, 1965; *Sex Is Between Two People* and *Days Ahead*, 1966; *Wandering*, 1966. Cafe La Mama—*Balm In Gilead*, 1965; *Sand Castle*, 1965; *The Rimers Of Eldritch*, 1966. Judson Poets Theatre—*Untitled Play*, 1968. Washington Theatre Club — *The Gingham Dog*, 1968 (also Broadway, 1969); *Serenading Louie*, 1970. Circle Rep—playwright in

residence; *Sextet (Yes)*, 1971; *The Great Nebula In Orion*, *The Family Continues* and *Ikke, Ikke, Nye, Nye, Nye*, 1972; *The Hot L Baltimore*, 1973; *The Mound Builders*, 1975; *Brontosaurus*, 1977; *The Fifth Of July*, 1978; *Tally's Folly*, 1979.

Awards: Drama Desk Vernon Rice Award—*The Rimers Of Eldritch;* New York Drama Critics and Obie Awards—*The Hot L Baltimore.*

ROBERT WILSON, *Playwright/Director*

Born: October 4, 1944; Waco, Texas

Director: Theatre Activity (Off-Off-Broadway), 1967; *ByrdwoMAN* (Off-Off-Broadway), 1968; *The King Of Spain* (Off-Broadway), 1969; *The Life And Times Of Sigmund Freud* (Brooklyn Academy Of Music), 1969.

Author/Director: *Deafman Glance* (Brooklyn Academy Of Music), 1971; *European tour*, 1971); *Program Prologue Now* (France, 1971; New York, 1972; Iran; 1972); *KA MOUNTAIN AND GUARDenia TERRACE* (Iran, 1972; New York, 1972); *The Life And Times Of Joseph Stalin* (Denmark, 1973, Brooklyn Academy Of Music, 1973); *A Letter For Queen Victoria* (Spoleto Festival, 1974; Broadway, 1975); *$ Value Of Many* (Brooklyn Academy Of Music 1975); *Einstein On The Beach* (European tour, 1976; Metropolitan Opera House, 1976); *I Was Sitting On My Patio This Guy Appeared I Thought I Was Hallucinating* (Off-Broadway), 1977; *Edison*, 1979.

Also: Founder (1969) Byrd Hoffman Foundation; designed sets and costumes for *Motel* (La Mama, ETC), 1965.

Awards: Obie Award (Special Citation)—*The Life And Times Of Joseph Stalin;* Vernon Rice Award—*Deafman Glance* (direction).

IRENE WORTH, *Actor*

Born: Nebraska

Theatre Companies: Old Vic — *Othello*, 1951; *A Midsummer Night's Dream*, 1951; *Macbeth*, 1952; *The Other Heart*, 1952; *The Merchant of Venice*, 1953; *Mary Stuart* (also Edinburgh Festival), 1958. Stratford (Ontario) Shakespeare Festival — founding member; appeared in *All's Well That Ends Well*, 1953; *Richard III*, 1953; *As You Like It*, 1959; *Hedda Gabler*, 1970. Phoenix Theatre—*Mary Stuart*, 1957. Royal Shakespeare Company — *Mac-*

beth, 1962; *King Lear*, 1962; *The Physicists*, 1963; *Tiny Alice*, 1970. Chichester Festival— *Heartbreak House*, 1967; *The Seagull*, 1973. National Theatre — *Oedipus*, 1968. Academy Festival Theatre—*Sweet Bird Of Youth*, 1975; *Misalliance*, 1976; *Old Times*, 1977; *After The Season*, 1978. Yale Repertory Theatre — *Prometheus Bound*, 1967. New York Shakespeare Festival — *The Cherry Orchard*, 1977; *Happy Days*, 1979.

Broadway: *The Two Mrs. Carrolls*, 1943; *The Cocktail Party*, 1950; *Toys In The Attic*, 1960; *Tiny Alice*, 1964; *Sweet Bird Of Youth*, 1974.

London: In addition to her work with theatre companies, London stage appearances include *The Time Of Your Life*, 1946; *The Play's The Thing*, 1947; *Lucrece*, 1948; *Native Son*, 1948; *Home Is Tomorrow*, 1948; *Edward My Son*, 1948; *The Cocktail Party* (Edinburgh Festival, 1949), 1951; *A Day By The Sea*, 1953; *A Life In The Sun*, 1955 (also Edinburgh Festival); *The Queen And The Rebels*, 1955; *Hotel Paradiso*, 1956; *The Ides Of March*, 1963; *Suite In Three Keys*, 1966; *The Seagull*, *Hamlet* and *Ghosts* (Greenwich Theatre season), 1974.

Also: Recitals —*Letters Of Love And Affection*, *Shakespeare's Sonnets*, *Venus And Adonis*, *Women Of Shakespeare*, poetry. Recordings — various Shakespeare plays including *Antony And Cleopatra*, Isak Dinesen's *The Old Chevalier*, excerpts from *Anna Karenina*.

Awards: Tony Awards — *Tiny Alice*, *Sweet Bird Of Youth;* Page One Award—*Toys In The Attic;* London Evening Standard Award — *Suite In Three Keys;* Variety Club Of Great Britain Award — *Heartbreak House;* Drama Desk Award — *The Cherry Orchard;* British Film Academy Award—*Orders To Kill;* Honorary Commander Of The Most Excellent Order Of The British Empire.

DESIGN
TYPOGRAPHY & PRODUCTION CO-ORDINATION
Durham Dodd, MGDC

EDITOR
Nancy Heller

PHOTOGRAPHER'S ASSISTANTS
Luke Wynne, Griffin Smith

RESEARCHERS
Michele Theriot, Stephen Morris

TYPESETTING
Expertype Graphics Limited

FILM PREPARATION & LITHOGRAPHY
Herzig Somerville Limited

BINDING
John Deyell Company

PAPER
West Vāco – Sterling Litho Gloss, 160M
Weyerhaeuser – Andorra Text, French Blue, 160M

BINDING MATERIAL
Columbia, Tanalin Ten

END PAPER
Strathmore – Grandee, Barcelona Grey, 80 Text

TYPEFACE
Souvenir

TECHNICAL DATA
Cameras: Nikon (35mm) Bronica (120mm) Sinar (4x5)
Film: Kodak Tri-X
Printing Paper: Ilford (Ilfobrom)